A HAUNTED HISTORY
OF PASCO COUNTY

A HAUNTED HISTORY OF PASCO COUNTY

MADONNA JERVIS WISE

Published by Haunted America
A Division of The History Press
Charleston, SC
www.historypress.com

Copyright © 2020 by Madonna Jervis Wise
All rights reserved

Cover: Photograph by Ernest E. Wise.

First published 2020

Manufactured in the United States

ISBN 9781467146814

Library of Congress Control Number: 2020938495

Notice: The information in this book is true and complete to the best of our knowledge. It is offered without guarantee on the part of the author or The History Press. The author and The History Press disclaim all liability in connection with the use of this book.

All rights reserved. No part of this book may be reproduced or transmitted in any form whatsoever without prior written permission from the publisher except in the case of brief quotations embodied in critical articles and reviews.

To Rachel, Mamie and Jervis

If history were taught in the form of stories, it would never be forgotten.
—*Rudyard Kipling*

CONTENTS

Preface	9
Acknowledgements	11
Introduction	13
1. Demise of 109	17
2. Dade City and Folklore: Haunted Inhabitants and the Like	21
3. Shroud of Misfortune on Lake Pasadena	61
4. Darby and Bradley Massacre Site Sits on Amusement Park	67
5. Land O'Lakes: From Stagecoach to Edward Scissorhands	70
6. Odessa and the Justice of Sheriff Bart	77
7. Crystal Springs Fountain of Youth and Surviving Extinction	84
8. Port Richey's Sacred Ground	87
9. New Port Richey: Fantasy and Silent Movie Legends	92
10. Zephyrhills: The Retired Civil War Colony and Its Legends	111
11. Wesley Chapel: The Feud and More	123
12. Lacoochee Lore	133
13. Trilby Tales	138
14. Moon Lake: The Dude Ranch	142
15. San Antonio: Rattlesnakes and Nuns	145
16. Ellerslie and Enterprise	148
Bibliography	151
About the Author	160

Preface

Open your perspective as you delve into the entries that follow! The places and folks are well researched. Based on primary and secondary sources, many of the mysteries included are based on written accounts or tales passed down from generation to generation. Primary sources in all historical accounts are viewed by the perception of the eyewitness.

From my earliest days, I sat at the feet of my grandparents and neighbors, mesmerized by the details of their life stories, most particularly the nuances of their daily lives that infused superstition, intuition and coincidence, as well as deep faith. As a lifelong educator, I employed experiential learning techniques used in the teaching of history—oral history, interviews, field trips and review of diaries and artifacts.

History is a multisensory experience. A childhood memory evokes an image, a smell, a nostalgic longing and an emotion. Often what lingers in a historical recollection is the sensory aspect of the experience. Enjoy this collection of stories about a diverse group of people and places that shaped Central Florida history.

Acknowledgements

Thanks to Margaret Beaumont, Scott Black, Sheryl Bryant, Jeff Cannon, Willa Bahr Chapman, Jamie Chastain, Dennis Cole, Ronnie Collins, William G. Dayton, Nicole Ferro, Shane Forrester, Erica Freeman, Leslie Gilmore-Lagosky, Billy Grant, Evan Green, Joe Gude, Kelly Hackman, Steven Herman, Brandie Kagey Hunter, Clinton Inman, Jeff Jeter, Ted Johnson, Buddy Jones, Bob Langford, Nick Linville, Joy Lynn, Susan Maesen, Cecil McGavern, Edith McGavern, Susan McMillian, Jeff Miller, Taylor Napier, Allan Near, Stephen Ove, Evie Parks, Derick Pontlitz, Linda Rodgers, Brian Schmit, Marco Stanley, Anna Stutzriem, Brian Swann, John M. Taylor, Danny Triplett, Bobbie Van Dercar, Irene Anne Westermann and Ernest E. Wise.

Introduction

With Historical Map and Discussion of History of the County and Florida

A *Haunted History of Pasco County, Florida*, conjures up images of misty, foggy, warm waters with unfolding enigmatic phantasmagorias that invigorate the imagination. It is a place where one squints for cognition of an object or aura and finds oneself hypnotically fantasizing over a fading horizon at a Gulf beach with its rhythmic tide rushing in and out. It's no wonder folklore of Florida is unique. The romantic land has long been sought after from a diverse and mesmerizing history that comes with numerous unique cultural origins, legends and lore. Mysterious legend and even haunted history come from as early as 10,000 BCE and run the gamut through indigenous culture, Spanish explorers, open range, homesteading as well as Seminole wars and the twentieth century with the Great Depression, Prohibition, moonshining and the development of communities.

The Land of Flowers holds magnetic appeal that stems from an enigmatic quest for the fountain of youth. In 1513, ruthless conqueror Ponce de Leon ironically named the area Land of Flowers. He had sailed with Columbus on his second expedition in 1493 and served as governor of the Spanish colony of San Juan (now Puerto Rico) and was ruthless in his treatment of Native Americans in the Caribbean. He sought out a contract in 1512 to look for the fountain of youth, and after making landfall around St. Augustine, he traveled down the peninsula to the Florida Keys. Later, when he returned to the area, the arrow of an indigenous warrior ultimately proved fatal. As you read the haunted history in Central Florida, you will see a pioneer's quest for a fountain of youth/healing as the account of Crystal Springs unfolds.

Introduction

Lithics recovered in Pasco County date from throughout the Paleo-Indian Period (14,000 BCE–8000 BCE), Archaic Period (8000 BCE–1000 BCE) and the Woodland Period (1000 BCE–900 CE), as well as artifacts from the Timucua (1000 BCE–900 CE), Tobago (900–1600) and Seminole (1750–present). Shane Forrester, a lifelong collector of Native American artifacts in central and eastern Pasco, explained that often lithics were repurposed over time from the most ancient of times to the Seminole. Similarly, in western Pasco, Herb Elliott, also a lifelong collector, has located thousands of stone artifacts. On the banks of his home near New Port Richey, the oldest were determined to be over ten thousand years old.

Dr. Jerald Milanich, author of *Florida Indians and the Invasion from Europe*, attempted to retrace the expedition of Hernando de Soto through Florida. From the Spanish documents he reviewed, he assumed that the expedition passed along a Native American trail in, or very near, present-day Dade City. It was here where the Spanish saw the first Native cornfields known as Plain of Guacozo. There is no conclusive evidence of which tribe the Spanish encountered; however, many Native groups across Florida were decimated by European-introduced diseases, leading to a population "vacuum" by the early eighteenth century. In the mid-eighteenth century, various southeastern Indians, the majority of whom were Creek, began settling in the area. They became known as the Seminole. Beginning in 1835, and until 1842, the United States and the Seminole were at war. Another war (the Third Seminole War, 1855–58) drove the Seminole from the region, encouraging further White settlement.

Make no mistake, Florida was a frontier, and the settlers who chose to come to Pasco County were hardworking and innovative. Gazing at historical archives, one cannot help but marvel at the pioneers—their tenacity, ingenuity and ability to withstand hardship and loss. The community of Pasco County was interrelated yet diverse. The stories collected from interviews and records capture anecdotes of Native Americans, Black workers in turpentine communities and railroads, farmers and cow hunters during open range and early entrepreneurs. In the burgeoning towns and villages there were scarce populations of settlers, and isolation was the norm. Only the Sunday church service or meeting at the general store brought them together. In that atmosphere, superstitions flourished, and family legends and rituals sprouted and were passed down.

A family was self-sufficient in handling every nature of life event from birth to burial. Loss was a common occurrence, and rugged subsistence life made sentimentality unviable, so rationalizations and traditions were born.

Introduction

Map of Florida in 1749, created by Robert de Vaugondy. *State Archives of Florida.*

Fighters and soldiers returning from skirmishes or conflicts like the Civil War had undefined melancholy that would be later named post-traumatic stress. It is little wonder that an array of ghost stories, supernatural tales and strategies for coping emerged that brought belief in enchantment, superstition and just plain dumb luck.

In the geographical journey through these tales, you will traverse local history from an original perspective. Through examination of recurrent ghost stories, weird coincidences, superstitions, dream premonitions and events that run the gamut from hilarity to tragedy, a new perspective of the history of Pasco County that reflects everyday humanity may emerge.

1
DEMISE OF 109

Carol Jeffares Hedman, reporter for the *Tampa Tribune*, unveiled intricate and riveting stories of local history in a 2003 article titled "Lawyer Has Ghost Story," about the most renowned ghost storyteller. She quipped, "When things go bump in the night, who do people call? Well, of course lawyer William G. Dayton," who collected and articulated age-old stories of ghosts and legends.

Major Francis Langhorne Dade and his troops camped along the Fort King Road near Pasco High School in Dade City on Christmas Day in 1835. After awakening, Dade confided that he had just experienced a mysterious dream that visibly upset him. He had seen images of deceased comrades from the War of 1812 marching hypnotically in front of him in precise formation. Prophetically, on December 28, Dade and his 108 soldiers were killed in an attack by Seminole Indians who waited in the palmettos near what is today Bushnell. The troops were marching from Fort Brooke to Fort King in Ocala, and the Seminoles led by Ote Emathla (who was known as Jumper) numbered about 180. The fatalistic ambush, later labeled the Dade Massacre, set off the Second Seminole War. One of only two survivors of Dade's troops recorded Dade's foretelling dream in his journal for posterity. Dayton said the hillside where Major Dade camped just south of Dade City is linked to a great deal of mystery and is the site for not only Dade's dream but also ghosts and mysteries that have spanned over a hundred years.

The site of the Dade Massacre in 1835 is commemorated at Dade Battlefield Historic State Park with a marker at the location where Major Dade fell in battle. *Ernest E. Wise.*

North of Dade City, where the original Fort King Road crossed the Withlacoochee River was the site where the U.S. Army post commemorating the Dade Massacre was established in 1836.

In March 1837, Thomas S. Jesup and Jumper met at Fort Dade and signed the capitulation to end the fighting, with the Seminoles supposedly agreeing to be relocated in Oklahoma Territory. The agreement was signed at Fort Dade because of its proximity to where Dade's troops were massacred. The Indians slipped away from the camp into the wilderness. A component of the capitulation was a validation for the arrest of Chief Osceola and other Seminole leaders. Chief Osceola died in 1838, dejected from the capture.

As it was sacred ground from 1835 forward, Dade Battlefield State Park was created in 1921. Park rangers conduct a haunted trail tour during late October, and reenactor events are commonplace. Guests, paranormal hunters and history buffs report strong emotions and energy that run the breadth of mirages from angelic figures to white smoke to black powder weapons and even an occasional sighting of Major Dade himself.

Historian Dayton, who shared the stories of the ghostly encampment, had not heard of haunted encounters at the battlefield park but retorted, "If there are ghosts, they would surely be there."

Fort Dade–Déjà Vu

Several Fort Dade locations emerged over time. At least three fort sites and a town site bear the name. The first fort site researched by historian Frank Laumer was built by the army in 1837 at the banks of the Withlacoochee near Lacoochee. It was a refuge location for settlers who needed protection from Indian attacks. A second Fort Dade was built by the Seventh Infantry in 1849, just south of Dade City, where Major Dade stopped to camp on the haunted hill during his final journey. A third location was at Egmont Key in 1882 for the Spanish-American War in response to fears that the Spanish would attack the coastlines.

Even more confusing in the Fort Dade naming was the village that grew from the prosperous homestead of James Gibbons near Lock Street, which was named Fort Dade. By 1884, it was surveyed as a town and populated by early merchants.

When the railroads arrived, merchants relocated out of necessity to be near the source of transportation. The town of Dade City emerged, although some settlement at the Fort Dade Village remained. Historians of Daughters of the American Revolution, such as Dorothy Lock and Ruth Embry Touchton, long argued that the town of Dade City had an identity crisis and might have more accurately been named Fort Dade.

2
Dade City and Folklore

Haunted Inhabitants and the Like

The settlement that was initially named Fort Dade had the lure of resources such as the Withlacoochee River and Fort King Road. With the unique origin of Pasco County, a process of selection of the county seat emerged in an election in 1889. When the dust settled, Dade City won with 432 votes over Gladstone, 205; Pasadena, 96; Urbana, 20; Clear Lake, 2; Jefferson, 2; and Owensboro, 1. Dade City developed the ambiance of a pre–Civil War southern town but maintained a population with a strong work ethic and frontier practicality.

Pasco County was established from a region of Hernando County on June 2, 1887, by Governor Madison S. Perry. Government affairs were conducted in a frame building owned by Henry W. "H.W." Coleman and William N. "W.N." Ferguson, which was used until 1889, when a permanent wooden courthouse was erected. In 1909, it was replaced by a domed brick structure that is still in use today. This historic courthouse holds a plethora of history and folklore, as does the county seat that served as the powerbase of the now burgeoning area from its selection as county seat in the 1889 election until about 1980, when the population and industrial base shifted from east Pasco to west Pasco and the New Port Richey area.

Architect Edward C. Hosford of Georgia drew blueprints for the majestic building, as he had designed courthouses throughout Florida, Georgia and Texas. Mutual Construction Company erected the courthouse with local architect Artemus Roberts as supervisor. In over one hundred years of service, the courthouse has housed events, meetings and numerous trials of

Painting interpretation of the 1909 Pasco County Courthouse with the previous wooden courthouse structure at left. *Clinton Inman.*

every nature, both civil and criminal. As one traverses the winding stairs, it is easy to contemplate the folks whose fates have been altered in the house of justice.

Growing pains of the 1909 structure grace the minutes of commission meetings. William Dayton recalled an incident in 1970. As he entered the front door, he heard the clerks remarking, "That poor dear elderly couple—they must have been terrified—trapped in that 1940s elevator for two hours." Eventually, the elevator restarted on its own accord.

With a 1940s renovation, a beam that supported the third floor was compromised and periodic pressure would occasionally halt the elevator. "The top floor was supported by the balcony, which was removed, and it sagged—even books on the third-floor law library regularly flew off shelves," said Dayton.

Other reports of the cantankerous elevator persisted over time and aggravated a case or two of claustrophobia. A 1979 *Tribune* article titled "The Day the Elevator Stuck" conveyed a calamity. "Stay calm," somebody hollered. Fifteen people had jammed themselves into the elevator to take a ride from the first floor to the second. While the contraption was suited to haul two thousand pounds, it hoisted the ample crowd a couple of feet past the second floor and was abruptly wedged in place. The frantic county workers, unable to locate the maintenance crew, pried open the doors with some makeshift tools and assisted the group in crawling out safely.

Among townsfolk who met their destinies in that remarkable courthouse with defining rulings and condemnations was Grace Maud Karney Evans. The ghostly quintessence form of dear Grace has been glimpsed, perhaps imagined, in ethereal form with an object. Could it be the scales of justice? Her presence is said to be one of a few guiding spirits that visit. She, like Lady Justice, subtly urges jurors and officials in leadership to weigh all factors and listen with quiet prudence.

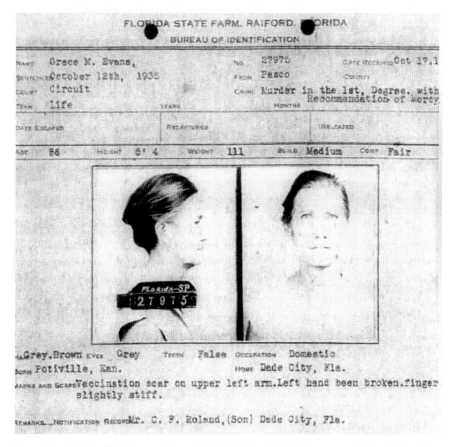

Grace Evans's identification card from Raiford Prison. *Florida Department of Corrections.*

Grace exhibited poise and gentle composure in five court appearances in 1935, when she was convicted of murder. She had chosen to survive in the midst of unthinkable abuse from two men in an era when women were to be seen and not heard. She was also sentenced by twelve men and then served twelve years of a life sentence, where she honed skills as a nurse and attended her fellow inmates. In 1965, a full pardon was granted. During her 1935 prehearing, grand jury indictment, trial and sentencing, the iconic structure was being renovated by the Works Progress Administration, a brainchild of President Franklin D. Roosevelt.

So, as Grace heard the testimony against her and stared blankly at her judge and jurors, she stated that she would accept her fate and walk to the gallows because she acted only to save her own life, and in what was reported as quiet submission of her fate, Grace sat perusing the progress of the craftsmanship and appeared to pray for justice. Attendance at her trial was record-breaking. After parole in 1947, Grace led a long and productive life and passed away in Dade City at the age of ninety-six. She didn't talk of this period of her life, but since her death in 1973, the faint illusion of a creature with the scales of justice who could be any number of ghostly tenants is sporadically seen as she descends the winding staircases at the 1909 courthouse. Rumor has it that Grace approves of the renovations orchestrated by Commissioner Sylvia Young that were completed in 1999.

COLEMAN AND FERGUSON, GENERAL STORE EXTRAORDINAIRE

Indicative of the commitment of merchants who moved from the original Fort Dade site and adapted to meet the growing needs of the burgeoning frontier town, Henry W. Coleman and William N. Ferguson ventured to Florida from Georgia and purchased a lot in the original section of town from Reuben Wilson. It was the second general store; the first had been built by W.C. Sumner. They opened the store ten days after construction began. Over the years, they occupied several different Meridian locations.

Mrs. D.E. Sumner wrote about the duo in 1934 in a letter that was published in the local newspaper, the *Dade City Banner*:

> Their store (Coleman-Ferguson's) was first located in Old Town near the present site of the Ice and Power plant. It was a huge one-story building about one hundred and fifty feet long. The people in Sumter, Hernando as

Coleman and Ferguson Store. *State Archives of Florida.*

Dade City. *J. Thomas Touchton.*

well as Pasco County all thought them foolish, the idea of such a big store in this neck of the woods. The goods began to arrive by the time the roof was on the building. In a few days that store was filled with merchandise of all kinds at first, except bolt cloth goods and ladies' dress goods. I have heard them say many times they just did not have room and time to bother with that class of merchandise. However, they had plenty of all other stock. They had a long rack built through the center of the store from front to rear; the rack held saddles of all kinds, bridles and harness and red virgin wool blankets for cattle men, cow whips, etc. This was to supply the cattle men trade. Also, they had a complete stock of buggies, fine harness wagons, both one and two horse. They had guns of all dimensions, mostly muzzle loaders, as people in those days purchased black powder and shot and gun caps and did the loading with ram rod. I will say, however, the old deer hunter always brought home the bacon those days.

Coleman and Ferguson spawned a business dynasty in the quaint town, and they possessed enormous political power. One of their slogans boasted of dry goods, guns and coffins. Coleman and Ferguson did eventually own and operate a funeral business as well as their general store, but in the early days, the general store was the meeting place and the provider of a motherload of resources, including caskets.

Death was commonplace in the 1800s and was attended to by the nuclear family, who was apt to suffer the agonizing loss of infants, young children and young mothers in childbirth. Two hundred of every one thousand infants died in the 1800s.

Diseases that would be prevented by antibiotics in the twenty-first century wrought painful loss on the frontier. In 1887, Dade City opted to quarantine itself from the rampant yellow fever outbreak in Tampa. Common practice with epidemics was to treat the sick in quarantine or block any potential victim from entering town, and in 1887, fear ran rampant. The county commission formed a vigilante committee to stand guard at the train depot. No one was allowed to get off the train in Dade City for fear that they would bring the disease. Any tourist who entered on foot or buggy was driven back to the train. Years later, it was discovered that the disease was not spread from human contact but by mosquitoes.

Reflecting on death and burial customs of frontier Florida families in the nineteenth century, Pasco County practiced important rituals that grew out of necessity. Some of these derived from myth and observances that were passed down in families and brought to Florida from the many origins of the settlers.

They chopped the cypress tree and hewed out the modest coffin or, if able, purchased a casket from their local store, such as Coleman and Ferguson. The circuit preacher was summoned for the service, and the family conducted in-home services. These affairs hatched graphic memories in children, leading to fear and superstition.

Researchers have found that as far back as 60,000 BCE, humans were burying their dead with ritual ceremony using flowers. The early practices were to appease the spirits who were thought to have caused or contributed to the death. There was a real fear of ghosts. The eyes of a beloved relative were closed not just for aesthetics but also because it was believed that gently caressing the eyelids to give the appearance of sleep would close off the spirit world to the living, as the common belief was that gazing into the eyes of a corpse would open a portal to one's own demise. The practice was to carry the coffin from the house feet first to prevent the spirit from beckoning another family member. Mirrors were taken down or covered so that the spirit would not be trapped and unable to pass to the great beyond. Photographs were hidden or frames turned down so spirits would not cling to impressionable family members. Graves were always oriented so that the bodies were placed with the head to the west and the feet to the east, as it was surmised that final judgment would come from the east. Practices of positioning furniture often took on a similar nature, and beds were generally positioned in a north–south position for luck. Doors were left unlocked, and windows were left open to ensure that the soul would not be obstructed in its migration to heaven.

Out of necessity, tombstones were often wooden and handmade. The concept of the tombstone originated from the belief that the ghosts needed to be weighed down. Many believed the paths to and from the cemetery in the funeral procession should differ so that the ghost would not be able to follow them home. Gun salutes, chanting songs and funeral bells were used to scare away ghosts at the cemetery grounds.

There were a number of enslaved people in Pasco County in the turpentine communities and on plantation-type farms. They incorporated traditions from Africa that included placing items on the grave, such as cooking utensils. Pipes were sometimes driven into the ground and used as speaking tubes for communicating with the deceased.

Until the early 1900s, women did most of the preparation for memorials in the home, including washing and dressing the loved one and displaying the body in the home. Some affluent homes had parlors that had been constructed with the practice of a wake or funeral of family members

Interior of a parlor at Coleman and Ferguson house. *Pioneer Florida Museum & Village.*

in mind. The fancy parlor was equipped with the finest of the family's belongings—portraits, furniture, piano and treasured objects. Kept clean and secluded, it offered ample space for the casket. Some houses were even constructed with a death door that led to the outside, as it was not considered appropriate to move the body through the house door.

Embalming did not begin until the Civil War, so tales of burying people alive spurned horrors and fears. Mary Todd Lincoln, for example, requested her body be laid in state for a number of days before actual burial to ensure she was indeed dead. Bells and even apparatuses in the coffin were also used to ensure that someone in a deep coma was not mistakenly buried alive. The rituals and practices provided fodder for ghost tales.

The Elegant 1912 Edwinola Hotel Oozes with Whodunits

Taylor Napier wrote in 2020, "My mother worked at the Edwinola when she was younger and she swore up and down that the place was haunted. The elevator would open on its own and you could see ghosts of women on some of the floors. Anytime I pass the building, I get chills."

Dade City's genteel and famous hotel is said to be inhabited by a number of ghostly apparitions. The original developer and owner, Seymour H. Gerowe, was killed in 1911, when he fell from a third-story window during construction of the majestic structure with Doric columns, wraparound porches and a mansard roof. Immediately following Gerowe's untimely death, his widow sold the unfinished hotel to Gerowe's brother-in-law Edwin and his wife, Lola Gasque, who completed it and named it after a combination of their own first names, with no mention of Gerowe. The formal opening of the hotel marked the premier social gala of 1912. Folks in their graceful attire, even occasional millinery couture, dined, danced and celebrated at the landmark.

Seymour is believed to be an occasional phantom there, as his idea for the dramatic hotel was erased when his life was cut tragically short from the accidental plunge off the third floor. Guests and workers such as Taylor's mother have reported eerie activities at the vintage hotel now used as a retirement home. Soft ghostly murmurs come from empty rooms, and the faint smell of cigar smoke rises from former dining areas. Folks working the night shifts have reported that a feminine ghost moves about the floors, but when she is spotted, she quickly vanishes.

The story of Mrs. Robert S. Braswell in 1916 may also intertwine with the mysterious persona of the Edwinola. She had an alleged encounter on June 30, 1916. In the fervor of Jim Crow laws and the period of the so-called Great Migration, in which thousands of Black people left the South, she had an encounter with a young Black man who was passing through town and stopped to ask her for a glass of water. She was the attractive young wife of the town photographer and lived just two houses away from the jail where the sheriff's quarters were located, which would fuel controversy among the citizenry and annoy the sheriff.

The *Dade City Banner* reported that at four o'clock in the afternoon, an unknown Black man entered a house in the neighborhood of the county jail and assaulted a White lady. "Tensions ran high tonight and armed parties are scouring every nook of the woods for miles around with men posted at every railroad crossing and every public road and swamp guarded. Blood hounds have been sent for."

Officials were unable to locate the alleged assailant. A reward of $650 was posted by the *Tampa Morning Tribune* on July 28, and anonymous notices were sent to the Black community telling them to "Get Out of Town." It so happened that a labor recruiting agency was in town from Connecticut offering work for $2 per day, and a few Black families did leave. Reporting

Edwinola Hotel. *Public domain.*

Edwinola Hotel photograph by Fred W. Kenfield, 1926 postcard. *Helen Eck Sparkman collection.*

of the tragic situation ended abruptly after this, and town lore intimates that a man was publicly lynched at Edwinola Park while a few traveling salesmen watched from the porch of the Edwinola Hotel. Although nobody was ever charged for the lynching and the alleged perpetrator of the attempted assault on Mrs. Braswell was never apprehended, this provides more fodder for yet another ghostly presence at Edwinola Park.

As for the 1916 lynching, historian Dayton says that it is not confirmed, but he feels reasonably sure it happened, although another version of the story has circulated. The tradition was to lynch the accused as close to the scene of the crime as possible, and it would explain the end of the search.

Susie Higgs

By Erica Freeman

On a summer's day in 1894, Susie Higgs arrived at her house in a Black neighborhood near Dade City. A gentleman sat beside her, driving the horse cart. Her husband, Milton Higgs, spotted them and shouted, "Get out!" He yanked her out of the vehicle by the collar and dragged her into the house.

The *Pensacola News* said that he subsequently "blew her brains out with a pistol." Within days, law enforcement caught him. Susie's death wasn't mourned in the press, as the same newspaper wrote, "The woman had a bad character." Black people bore the brunt of sensationalistic journalism. Just four years later, buffalo soldiers stationed in Tampa lamented "the sensational and distorted publicity lavished upon 'every little thing' done by them."

Just one month after Higgs's death, the corpse of Abe McGirt was discovered near Trilby. Not only was his neck broken, but his skull was also smashed, and a bullet was found in his chest. "Family problems" led law enforcement to suspect his stepsons and charge them with the murder.

By October, Milton Higgs shared his sentencing with Zelina McGirt, Lewis Raymond, Will Mitchell and Henry Morris. Zelina and the other three men had colluded in the murder of Zelina's husband, Abe. All five were sentenced by Judge Barron Phillips to hang in Dade City. The *Weekly Tribune* described McGirt's murder as "the most foul, coldblooded murder ever committed in the state." However, many were convinced that Henry Morris was innocent.

In May 1895, Morris was a free man. Zelina McGirt, Raymond and Mitchell had their sentences changed to life imprisonment. This sounds like a blessing, but they were more valuable alive as prisoners. In the aftermath of slavery, Florida had found the next means of plentiful, cheap labor: inmates, mostly Black. By 1877, inmates were leased to private companies and industries for everything from fruit picking to phosphate mining. In 1915, Florida had new needs and used its convenient labor force to build roadways such as Highway 301 and, ironically, the workcamp that would become a state prison, Zephyrhills Correctional Institution.

Just one block north of the Edwinola lies the former Dade City Jail. It witnessed six hangings between 1892 and 1917. The gallows on the west side of the building are now an office, and the entire building was converted to civilian use. One of those hangings appears to be Milton Higgs. Susie and Abe are buried somewhere in Pasco in unmarked graves, possibly at Trilby.

Sunnybrook Tobacco Meets Its Demise through Fire, Hurricane and Disease

Sunnybrook Tobacco Company cultivated shade-grown tobacco, primarily for the Sumatra leaf used for cigar wrappers. It eventually vanished without a trace, as the crops were hit by an outbreak of black shank disease, as well as a devastating fire at the company's facility in 1924, which left "the whole town smelling like a cigar for weeks." Dade City, like many locales in the 1800s, was periodically an unwitting location of illness and dread that could be, perhaps unknowingly, self-imposed. In an age when folks believed tobacco was a health-building supplement that would ward off disease and serve as a medicine, Dade City's Sunnybrook Tobacco Company was Pasco County's largest employer from 1908 until 1920.

As one reflects more than one hundred years later, the demise of the tobacco industry was as ghastly as the maladies inadvertently imposed on citizens who partook of the various practices of tobacco consumption, sometimes from their earliest childhood. In genealogy, the causes of death are identified on documents by terms we may not hear today, such as dropsy, grippe, vapors, hysteria, pleurisy, cholera infantum and fits. The lack of cause and effect in disease made health and illness subject to luck and misfortune. The prevalence of tobacco use certainly sent some of our ancestors to an

Workers at Sunnybrook Tobacco Farm in Dade City. *State Archives of Florida.*

earlier death than might have been dictated by heredity. The loss of jobs greatly impacted the community as well.

Black shank was first identified in Florida in 1924, and by 1966, the disease was in every major tobacco-growing county in the state. The root fungus causes the leaves to droop and nearly wiped out the crop in 1926. It remains in the soil for many years. In addition to the fire, in October 1921, the tropical storm often called the Tarpon Springs Hurricane, which impacted all of Pasco County, destroyed nine of the tobacco barns and 110 acres of the half-shade areas at a loss of $100,000.

Dade City's POW Camp

The World War II bandstand monument stands gloriously in the center square of Dade City and reflects the city's patriotism and prideful heritage of service. While brave soldiers were fighting in Europe and the South Pacific and folks in Pasco were recycling commodities and purchasing war bonds, Dade City assisted in another manner that was frightening to many. From 1942 to 1946, 250 prisoners of war were placed in a camp in Company 7 of Camp Blanding. Prisoners were German soldiers, many from Rommel's Afrika Korps, captured in North Africa. The newspapers reported, "Nazis were in Pasco County."

POWs were put to work and manufactured limestone bricks, built warehouses and assembled shipping boxes in Dade City and surrounding communities. Work locations included Pasco Packing, Cummer Sons Cypress Mill and McDonald Mine near Brooksville. Remnants of the barracks were torn down in the 1980s.

At the former sight of the German POW camp in Dade City, walk by slowly, and some say you will hear the faint whisper of *danke* or *auf wiedersehen* from the ghost of Arthur Lang. From Ommersheim, Germany, he was eighteen when he enlisted and was sent to the French front in 1944. He was later captured by the Americans and sent to England to be subsequently transported across the Atlantic. He remembered dodging the German

Dade City German prisoner of war camp in 1944. *Tampa Tribune.*

submarines en route and ultimately being held at the Dade City POW camp. He returned to visit Dade City in 1986.

Lang recalled, "I cannot tell you what it is for a young person to be behind barbed wire for a length of time. You just have to imagine and see how you feel."

Although most accounts of POW treatment at Company 7 were humane, after World War II ended, security at the camp increased, and the food supply plummeted. Lang recalled that a young lady brought baked goods to him and other prisoners. With language barriers, he struggled to communicate, but a lifelong regret was that he never thanked her for her kindness that allowed him to survive and hold on to hope for an end to the war. His goal in the 1986 visit was to find her and thank her, but he was unable to locate the kind soul.

Haunted School

Schools in the area date to Fort Dade Academy in the 1850s, but public education became more prevalent when the Pasco School Board was created in 1887. Educational institutions throughout the area owe gratitude to a teachers' certification program in the South Florida Normal School, which trained and certified teachers from around the state in Dade City. The traditions of formal education shape the character of the communities. School reunions, annuals and memories of sporting events are prominent in the repertoire of memories. The Pioneer Museum and Village in Dade City, and later the West Pasco Historical Society, participated in the Smithsonian grant project on Home Teams, and the author did extensive research on women in team sports in the schools and community throughout its history. The community produced some well-known figures such as Mudcat Grant and Jim Courier. As far as ghostly stories, it seems that one school in particular stands out.

The 1913 Pasco High School building faced College Street (named for the South Florida Normal Institute; it is now named Fourteenth Street) and was surrounded by pine trees and festooned with Spanish moss. Used for high school classes until 1949, when a new school plant opened across the street south of Howard Avenue, the building with a dramatic columned portico and exposed stairways hinted of an antebellum era.

At opening, the school board boasted that the two-story, fireproof structure offered four classrooms, a library, an office and a cloakroom on the first floor, while the second floor housed an airy auditorium that was dually used by

The 1912 Pasco High School building was said to be fireproof, with four classrooms on the lower floor and a large assembly room upstairs. It was in use until 1949. *Florida Pioneer Museum & Village.*

the community. Equipped with steam heat and running water, a secluded basement contained boilers and an indoor recreation room.

In the years before the iconic building (later locally known as the adult education office) was demolished in 2006, retired school administrator Nancy Rinck reported that the custodial workers regularly shared tales of a female ghost in a white, flowing, translucent dress who floated through the rooms at dusk. It was recounted that the faint echoing of her delicate footsteps was often discerned. Theories unfolded about the ghostly presence. Some believed it was a former student whose life was cut short by a sudden illness and sought to continue her studies, while others theorized that the ghost was that of a teacher who dedicated her life to the fold.

The high school building hosted a launch of local soldiers ready to be sent off to the Great War in 1917 with its brutal trench warfare and mustard gas. Many of these soldiers did not return from Europe and the war, and there is conjecture that the lady in white was a teenager whose fiancé was sent to Europe and succumbed to the treachery. Her lover did not return from the Great War, shaping a painful life experience for the lady in white who paces the area in painful acknowledgement of her bereavement and loss. Or could it have been that the custodians mistook some resident vermin who inhabited the building for over ninety years?

The Jailhouse

Some distance from the site of the old high school building at the northeast corner of Robinson Avenue and Tenth Street stands the 1892 Pasco jail building. On an occasional winter evening, folks claim they have heard the melodious phrasing or soft humming of "Swing Low, Sweet Chariot… coming for to carry me home" from the illusory voice of one Edgar London. The 1865 song penned by Wallis Willis, an enslaved man who reminisced about his life in Mississippi and spoke of the risk and potential freedom of the Underground Railroad, was inspiration for Edgar London. Edgar was riveted by the sound of the crowd of both loved ones and macabre spectators who softly chanted this lyric as he sauntered to the gallows to meet his fate. The jailhouse was an ominous place where picnickers situated themselves on the grounds for the spectacle of public hangings and where at least one unauthorized lynching occurred after a prisoner was seized from the jail. Stories of revenooers delivering jugs of moonshine to the jail and African American hymn songs on the grounds were abundant.

On that fateful day of December 17, while the noose was being adjusted around the neck of London, who had been convicted of killing his wife, the condemned displayed the utmost composure and was seen to be whispering a prayer. Sheriff Ike W. Hudson placed the black cap over his head and sprang the trapdoor. The enormous crowd, including families and children, sang the heartrending gospel song, emblazoning the atmosphere. After the hanging, Ike returned to his two-story house, which was affixed on the east side of the jailhouse. It was impossible for him to sleep that night as he recalled the events of the day. Undoubtedly, there were other attendees who were also haunted by the sight. Public hangings were abolished in Florida in January 1924.

The jailhouse stands proudly today. Buddy Jones has owned the building for several years. In an interview, Buddy said he would not admit to encountering the restless ghosts of condemned criminals who left the earth through the trapdoor of the hangman's platform. "If it is haunted, it is not haunted for me," Jones said with a smile. "I have been here late at night many times." Legends, however, abound. In 1984, *Tribune* reporter Rosemary Brown exposed a legendary tale from local Billy Stewart, a jail detainee who spent endless days staring out the prison bars, succumbed to death and is yet whispered to be seen periodically, peering from the window.

Considered the first masonry building in the county, it has original steel bars. In a 1999 interview with James Thorner for the *Times*, Jones related

The 1892 Pasco County Jail originally housed the gallows and the sheriff's living quarters. *Ernest E. Wise.*

a number of remarkable stories about the structure. Just after purchasing the building, Jones called his friend who owned a metal detector to look for artifacts. "One find made their hearts skip a beat, considering the building's violent past. It was a metal box full of bones. Jones said at first we were aghast, but they turned out to be animal bones," wrote Thorner.

The most frightening of hangings occurred in 1922, Thorner wrote, "The city's oral history still teems with stories of the hanging of Alonzo Tucker, convicted of murdering his girlfriend in the early 1920s." He was abhorred by townsfolks in particular because after the murder, he chopped up the girl's body and dumped it in one of the city's public wells. Horrified by the murder and the poisoning of one of the major sources of water, the town shunned Tucker. Not one local preacher would agree to accompany Tucker to the scaffold. That task fell to a German immigrant priest from St. Leo Abbey named Father Francis Sadlier.

Historian Dayton remembers tales of the hanging told by his late uncle, former city attorney George Dayton. George recalled sneaking out of his house as a boy of six in hopes of catching a glimpse of Tucker on his final walk. His mother nabbed him in the yard and locked him in his bedroom with an admonition that hangings were not suitable pastimes for little boys. His childhood friend across the street, similarly locked in the house, made it to the execution after scampering down a tree limb from his bedroom window.

MERIDIAN MYSTERY MAN AT THE MERIDIAN APARTMENTS

In 1996, Jack Monday set out to restore the neglected Dade City Meridian Apartments by recruiting contractor Doyle Ray from Seffner who had experience in historical renovation from Tampa's Hyde Park. They converted the eight one-room apartments to six units and kept original features like the quaint fireplaces. Ray commented in a 1996 *Times* article written by Jeffrey Brainard that the foot-thick exterior walls made of layers of concrete, brick, tile and mortar were built to last. When it opened on July 11, 1925, it was advertised as the "first modern apartment building" located on the corner of Meridian and Twelfth Street. "Entering the building one stepped into a broad hallway which extended the length of the building…with easy stairways from both front and rear. Fittingly enough the first family to locate within its walls is that of Mr. and Mrs. Frank P. Allen, under whose supervision the building was erected." The apartments were a classic example of boom-time architecture from the 1920s.

Charles T. Bowen included the apartments in his Halloween exposé on October 31, 1995, titled "Ghost Tales Never Hurt the Bottom Line," in which he speculated that the town may be cashing in on the trend for ghost tours. Director of Main Street Gail Hamilton quipped in response that it was not a bad idea to add ghost stories to the Monster Mash fundraiser, summarizing, "There's plenty of material in Dade City for ghost tours."

Bowen wrote, "There's a lot of banging noise echoing around the Meridian building. It's Halloween so the ghost of a bygone era is returning to the 1920s apartment building two blocks from downtown." The banging, of course, originated from workers on the renovation who were moving interior walls and either scaring away the ghosts or disturbing them. "Strange sights are part of the two-story building's past. The smashed-out windows and empty insides certainly give it a haunted appearance. The ghost story involves the Meridian Mystery Man, once spied by a youngster playing next door. The child looked up and saw the man in a corner window at the rear of the building," wrote Bowen.

Meridian Apartments. *Ernest E. Wise.*

"Building owner Monday replied, 'It was probably some harmless old man who lived there, but the kid next door didn't know that. Like in the movie, *Home Alone.*'"

THE HAUNTED HILL AND THE MOST NOTORIOUSLY HAUNTED HOUSE IN DADE CITY

Herbert Stockton Massey Jr.'s House

The hillside where Dade and his troops camped on their fateful journey in 1835 surfaces periodically in the haunted history of the area. Dayton clarified in a 1989 interview that the stories seemed to indicate that the hillside itself held the enchantment; the area is along U.S. 301, south of town, and now houses the Hillside Trace apartments and a Florida Medical Center building.

The late Martha Cochrane, who Dayton said was not one to make things up, told him that when she was a girl in the 1890s Colonel J.A. Hendley recalled being thrown from his horse while riding on that very hillside that was abundant with tall pines. (Martha was in a position to hear the latest. Born in Dade City and a lifelong resident, she owned a boardinghouse for many years. She passed away in 1991 at the age of eighty-eight.) Hendley, a respected attorney and legislator, said he encountered a woman in a long white dress. The apparition vanished but spooked the horse. He was known for his equestrian prowess, and all were astonished that Hendley would lose his seat and break an arm from the fall. Dayton chuckled, however, as he recalled the story. "There was conjecture that the colonel, who was a renowned horseman, might have fallen from the horse on his own account and perhaps concocted, or at least embellished, the tale to cover a twinge of embarrassment."

In the 1900s, a couple of houses were built on the haunted hillside, including Stockton Massey's. He reportedly had plenty of occasions to think his house was haunted. In a recent interview, Dayton shared his recollections. There were many accounts. During a cocktail party, an out-of-town guest strolled through the garden, went back inside and asked who the woman was in the old-fashioned, long, white dress. No one else saw her.

On another occasion, hosting some friends with a young child, Dayton himself witnessed the three-year-old toddler walking into the sitting room

The haunted hill now houses Hillside Trace apartments. *Ernest E. Wise.*

with his hand posed in such a manner that it appeared he was holding the hand of an imagined person who was leading him through the wall. Dayton theorized that the perceived floorplan predated the remodeling of the house, and the ghost was moving about the former rooms with the child in tow. Dayton explained that the house had been erected around 1900 and was purchased by the Massey family, and subsequently, extensive remodeling had been completed.

On yet another occasion, Dayton articulated that he saw some neighbors approach Stockton's house with a dog. The pooch jumped out of the pickup, sniffing the ground as dogs do, and then came bounding up, barking in a panicked manner as he approached the back door. Then the canine froze with sheer terror, and his hair bristled visibly while his panicked eyes were somewhat transfixed. Massey casually remarked, "Oh that is just the ghost. Dogs can see it, and people can't."

Dayton added that after Massey died, he was asked by a local resident whether he concurred that the deceased believed in ghosts. He responded, "People who live in haunted houses usually do."

In 1986, popular *Times* reporter Jan Glidewell, known for his courageous and sometimes unconventional research, decided to do some ghostbusting on his own at the Massey house. Walking through the charred remains of the house that had been damaged in a 1981 fire, he spied a paperback novel titled *Death of a Ghost* (presumably the edition by Margery Allingham) lying open and facedown as if half-read. When he scanned the page, he noticed the underlined passage, "And if you see a strange old lady mingling with the guests on one of these occasions, treat her with respect. It will be my ghost in disguise."

Glidewell and his buddy, *Times* photographer Jim Stem, selected Dade City's "most haunted house" to spend the entire night. Glidewell explained in his research that a "lady in white" legend about the ghost on the hill in south Dade City had been around for a little less than a century. The legend had it that the lady in white was about thirty and was a survivor of an age-old Indian massacre.

The home was owned for years prior to its demolition by Stockton Massey, who said he was informed that the ghost first turned up at a séance around 1900 but refused to reveal the name of the sole surviving participant of the séance to Glidewell, chuckling that it might prevent them from hiring another babysitter.

The *Tribune*, on June 1, 1988, printed an exposé on H. Stockton Massey Jr., titled "Eccentric Left Behind a Trail of Controversy," and shared an overview of his unique life. Born in 1930, he was heir to one of the largest fortunes in the area and came from a family that dated to 1912, when his grandfather George B. Massey, an executive for the Sunnybrook Tobacco Company, moved his family from Ohio. Over time, the businesses turned to land and citrus, and Massey founded the Pasco Packing Association with three other partners. Soon after, he was appointed by Governor LeRoy Collins to the state citrus commission. "The Masseys were a gracious 'old school' southern family," said Dayton. "You might call them planter class."

With the enormous wealth, Massey became something of a personality about town, with a streak of cynical nonconformity. He dressed in white shirts with European-style ties and believed in reincarnation and ghosts, including the one that reportedly haunted his home. "He believed firmly in George Wallace, reincarnation and ghosts, including the one that reportedly haunted his home…and became a Dade City legend."

Massey, his friends say, so loved dramatic gestures and histrionic poses that no one knew whether to take him seriously. "He enjoyed being seen as eccentric," Dayton said to the *Tribune*. "It was a style deliberately cultivated. You never could be sure when he was being serious. He wasn't averse to exaggerating his tragic background."

Stockton Massey's house, located on the haunted hill south of Dade City, had an extensive history of eerie events. *Photo by Jim Stem, courtesy of* Tampa Bay Times/*ZUMA Wire.*

The August 15, 1981 blaze that overtook the house was not without suspicion. According to investigative records, associates of Massey heard him comment at various times that he hoped the house would burn because it was evil and haunted by the spiritual remnant of the woman killed near the site, relating that the ghost regularly opened and closed doors and had even turned the stove on and off.

When the building was destined for demolition, Glidewell and Stem obtained permission to explore the place. Glidewell stated, "As night wore on and Stem and I exhausted our stock of rehashed ghost stories, it became apparent that nothing was going to happen and nothing did….Real students of the paranormal will insist that we did half a dozen things wrong, and that, anyway, the failure of a ghost to appear on one given night does not mean it doesn't exist."

Annetta's Attic

Perusing the shelves and displays of an antique shop is analogous to devouring an intricate Victorian novel. Each plate, book or novelty has a make-believe story. What tiny person might have worn those buckle shoes? Look at the intricacy of the crochet pattern. What era would this have come from?

Janis Annetta Gore's shop opened in 1983 at 14136 Eighth Street. It featured a whopping twenty-two rooms of antiques. The shop closed in 2018, and the community lost eighty-seven-year-old Annetta on January 2, 2018. She had been in the antique business for fifty years and was a certified appraiser.

It is difficult to know where the spirits that were observed in the attic rooms of the shop came from. Did they arrive at the shop with emotional baggage, so to speak? Or perhaps it was the aged Huckabay building.

Dayton said Gore shared with him that mysterious things happened in the attic shop rooms. On more than one occasion, she and her employee unlocked the door to notice that displays were altered and items had been shifted around. The lady who worked for her had seen the vision of a man standing in the hallway who startled her, and when she moved back around to catch another look, he vanished.

Taylor Napier remembered, "My dad used to deliver Pepsi a few years back and enjoyed visiting with the owners of Annetta's Attic, the antique shop. The owners said they thought a spirit of a young girl lived on the

Annetta Gore's Antique Shop on Eighth Street. *Danny Triplett.*

second floor where they kept children's toys. They said customers thought toys occasionally moved or made noise that would startle you. The owners even experienced it too."

Dayton's law office was in the same restored building, and although he never experienced ghostly encounters, he remembered a former occupant of the building, whose office was on the second floor, telling him of several sightings accompanied by a sudden cold rush and a rattling doorknob.

Housed in the Huckabay building beside the Ole City Market Building, the attic was renovated in 2005. "Ain't this a great thing?" artist Jack Beverland exclaimed during the renovation. "What a story the walls of this store could tell you."

Contractor Larry Cole, walking down the creaking pine steps from the second floor, smiled and added, "The building is a work of art, too." A 2005 *Tribune* piece by Steve Kronacki stated that it possessed the spirit of turn-of-the-century Pasco—original red Georgia clay tile flooring and tan-colored bricks made from Withlacoochee River clay, which were fired down the road in Lacoochee in the late 1800s.

Barbara Huckabay was recognized for the renovation in a state award in 2006, and the building was used to house her grandfather Woots Huckabay's grocery store. The upstairs housed a lawyer's office. Those pine-floored, second-story offices had housed a dentist office, the military draft board during World War II and market storage for the grocery store. The aging pains of such a deep-rooted dwelling produced timeworn creaks and spawned mysterious reports over time.

816 South Fourteenth Street, Dade City

The Little Boy's House

Two Tampa-area reporters described the demise of the haunted house at 816 South Fourteenth Street known as the Little Boy's House. Charles T. Bowen penned, "Flames burned a South 14th Street house that was supposed to be haunted. Children called it 'the little boy's house.'…Only young children could see the ghost of a youngster who died after falling off a second-story porch and breaking his neck." Carol Hedman wrote, "Not much is left of the two-story house, reduced to a pile of bricks and ashes by an early-morning fire.…Bright yellow 'No Trespassing' sign sticks out among the charred remains of the turn-of-the-century house on 14th Street."

The house was built in 1903 across the street from the Pasco Middle School track. The oddly constructed two-story house had a door on the second floor that was boarded shut. The story goes that the owners' son fell from the porch and broke his neck in the 1920s. Devastated, his parents removed the porch and nailed the door shut. But for years after the couple left, children reported seeing a little boy in the second-story window.

The ghost of the little boy "was just as real as anything else to the young children in the neighborhood," said Dayton in a 2003 presentation to the Pasco County Historical Society at the American Legion Hall.

While talking with Dayton in 2020, he elaborated on the story. Visiting friends Amy and Carl Lendian, who lived near the house years ago, he first learned about the house. "As we sat visiting and watching the kids playing in the neighborhood, the story unfolded. Young tykes would spot a little boy standing in a second-story window of the house and ask why he didn't come join them. The fellow they described was around five years old and was as real as anything to them and would gaze out the window longingly when they were playing," Dayton said. Parents would brush off the account as an imaginary friend but found it peculiar as well. "On this visit, I heard them refer to the little boy's house. The perception was that the younger children, say six and under, seemed to see the little boy, while kids older than eight or nine, and certainly adults saw just an empty window."

Curious about the house, Dayton later walked through and explored the place when it stood empty and in disrepair. "The house had a mysterious door on the second floor…would open out but there was absolutely nothing. The place was quite rickety. There had been upright supports that were much wider than the usual. The entire house kind of shook if you

Rendition of Little Boy's House at 816 South Fourteenth Street as little boy looks longingly. *Clinton Inman.*

jumped up and down. It also had very shallow fireplaces that were made for narrow coal grates."

The Dade City Fire Department listed chimney maintenance as the cause of the fire and estimated the loss at $35,000 in 1989. Margaret Herrmann Beaumont remembered that the house was near Florida Avenue on South Fourteenth Street, and two houses were later constructed on the lot.

The owner of the house at the time of the fire was Darlene Bukszar, who purchased the vacant building in 1980. It was empty for several years before she purchased it. She was in the process of selling it to Brad Bartlett, who was living there when the fire broke out on November 25, 1989. Bukszar said she knew a little boy fell off the porch and died, but she never heard the stories about the ghost.

Hedman explained that the house was originally built by a doctor who owned the neighborhood, which was situated in orange groves. When he died, his family sold off parcels little by little. Bukszar said Joan Bennett was the next owner. She sold it to Thomas Frakes. Bukszar said she bought it from Frakes, and it had been vacant for several years. Dayton and Bukszar did not know who was living at 816 when the little boy died.

Hettie Spencer's House

The enchanted two-story 1904 Victorian gothic frame house on Meridian Avenue is known as the Hettie Spencer house. She was postmistress from 1897 to 1936. Dayton has since lived there for forty-five years.

Joe Gude, a third-generation Floridian whose family is known for kumquat growing, witnessed a surreal event at the Spencer house in 1992. He and a friend were guests at the house, enjoying an evening of stories with the best storyteller in town. An hour or two into the gathering, the storyteller excused himself to retrieve something from the kitchen/dining room area. Joe explained:

> *Within a few minutes we heard a thud of some type and scurried out to see what it might be. In the foyer between two open French doors lay Storyteller spread out on the floor and motionless with a cut on his hand that was bleeding. For several seconds, we found ourselves standing over him, one of us on each side looking down. "Are you all right?" we asked.*
>
> *In rhythmic response to our question, one of the French doors slammed violently shut in hurricane speed. We shrieked as there was no breeze. The other guest walked into the adjoining room to investigate if there was any explainable reason. The look on his face was sheer horror. He whispered there is nobody here with us.*
>
> *As Storyteller roused and was fine, we bandaged up his hand and exited as quickly as was possible.*
>
> *It was a good six months until we related the story to Storyteller, who agreed it was weird but explained that the dining room had been used as*

the invalid room of Hettie Spencer in her last days, and he hypothesized the door slamming was an angered and perhaps ghostly response to the invasion of her space.

Dayton also explained that on the first night he spent at the house, he discerned a few odd noises and, just to be safe, declared, "Mrs. Spencer, it is just me…Little Billy Dayton!"

Dayton said that folks have glimpsed an ethereal feminine ghost in a long white dress in the house. "When Dick Tombrink was courting his future wife, Margaret Louise Rice, he brought her over to my house." (Louise Tombrink was a revered teacher at the area high school for many years.) "They were sitting in the front room, and she said, 'Who is that upstairs?' Of course, Dick and I knew about the ghost stories." They replied that it was just the ghost.

House sitters also told Dayton that they'd seen the lady in white while he was out of town. They were in the backyard when they saw her peering out of the window. "I think they may have made that up for my amusement, or maybe for their own, and then started believing it," he said.

Hettie Spencer's house (*left*) at the northeast corner of Meridian Avenue and Eleventh and the Christopher and Lucy Lock house (*right*). *Helen Eck Sparkman collection.*

Dayton did experience a strange phenomenon while walking at dusk in his backyard. From the nearby vacant house, he heard women talking, reminding him of when he was a child and his mother's bridge club would gather. But no one was inside what was once the home of Laura Spencer Porter, a pioneer banker who was responsible, along with Frank Price, for the Bank of Pasco reopening after the 1926 collapse of Florida boom and the 1929 stock market crash. They had insisted on repaying bank depositors, none of whom incurred a loss. She also happened to be the sister of Hettie Spencer. Chuckling, Dayton recalled that the ladies, Hettie, Laura and his mother, used to go to church choir practice and then partake in a game of bridge. Maybe the gang of lady ghosts was continuing the practice, he said.

Bowen, in his *Tribune* article "Ghost Tales Never Hurt the Bottom Line," referenced an interview with Jack Richards of Ghost Talk, Ghost Walk in Savannah about why people believe in ghosts. Richards explained that it was human nature and fascination with eternity. This caused Bowen to further contemplate what the people who had done the research believed, so he inquired of Dayton, who replied, "I've never seen a lady in white. I've never seen a ghost....Don't want to, either."

A real history buff, Joe Gude served on the board at the Pioneer Museum & Village for a number of years. Gude was given the task of locking the John Calhoun "J.C." Overstreet House for an occasional event. "There were a number of stories about that house," said Gude, who recalled a story imparted to then curator Donna Swart and him. Peering longingly out one of the upstairs windows was the waiflike figure of an elegant lady. Perhaps Mary Strickland Overstreet, J.C.'s first wife who passed away soon after the death of their teenage son, was reminiscing. The tragic death of their son was referenced in J.C.'s obituary in 1922: "This son with all the promise of the future met tragic death."

J.C. fought with the Florida Volunteers in the Civil War and homesteaded eighty acres on a spectacular hill in 1883. His elegant house was used for boarding settlers arriving to the area. J.C. married again at age sixty to lovely Annis Middlebrook, and they had two children, John Park Overstreet and Albee Overstreet, the latter of whom was born in the Overstreet house on December 4, 1896.

Dade City's Own Version of Miss Havisham on Church Street

Captain Frederick L. Bridge was a Union officer during the Civil War. "It was cause for strong bitterness among the crackers. Those who knew the Bridge family had stories about the manner in which prejudice against them was displayed," explained Dayton. Bridge presented a stern countenance and was a highly cultured and literate man. He subscribed to a number of literary magazines and was liberal in his thinking.

"Walking down the streets, folks were known to cross over to the other side to avoid walking in front of the Bridges' home. Families cautioned children to stay clear of the captain. Kids said he was apt to give you the evil eye," related Dayton.

The Bridge home was directly across the street from the Presbyterian church on Church Street. In the twenty-first century, Church Street Historic District, between Ninth and Seventeenth Streets, covers fourteen acres and contains thirty-four historic buildings. The community hosts a Christmas street during a designated week in December, with all the houses decorated and the numerous churches hosting singing celebrations. It is a place that livens Christmas spirit. The captain's only daughter, Winifred "Winnie" L. Bridge, an accomplished artist, writer and photographer, was born before her time in many ways. She would have loved Church Street Christmas and had a great deal to contribute.

Geoffrey Pounds penned a review of Winnie for a July 28, 1980 piece. He stated, "In her eighty-one years, Winnie came to know death, and disease, prejudice and ridicule, love and lost love. But she also came to know the beauty of a painted picture, the fascination of a photograph, and the joy of teaching young and eager minds."

The house held many secrets in its day and served as an artist's haven for Winnie, an accomplished teacher who, in other circumstances, would have been heralded for her writing, painting and photography.

The strongest influence in Winnie's life was her beloved father. Winnie penned his 1922 obituary, which said, "He served in the army from the time he was sixteen years old until the Civil War was over....He went into service a strong young boy and came out a physical wreck." After the war, he struggled with his health, particularly lung ailments, and was forced to move his family from Maine to Georgia and then eventually Florida. By the time Frederick passed away in May 1922, he had earned a place in the community, as the *Dade City Banner* wrote, "Three War Heroes Die within a

Church Street as it appeared in early days. *Helen Eck Sparkman collection.*

Prolific artist Winifred L. Bridge's drawing shows four women symbolically studying a young man in miniature. *Susan Maesen.*

Day" and profiled two union soldiers and one Confederate soldier, with the statement that their loss "had cast a shadow over the city."

An accomplished woman, Winnie had strong opinions about women and working and kept a meticulous diary that was donated to the Florida Pioneer Museum & Village. She contributed poems to local publications and painted magnificent watercolor and oil paintings. Her photographs are in several historical collections.

Dewey Hudson said he was one of her students in second grade in 1906. "She is not hard to remember. She was so refined and polished, she stuck out that way. She was an excellent teacher and an elegant lady."

As the only child, Winnie lovingly cared for her father and, after his death, nursed her mother, Katherine, for several years. With these obligations, she wasn't able to court and marry like her peers. In her fifties, she married Presbyterian minister C.W. Latham, who passed away three years later. Her diaries detailed her loneliness, and in the last years, she enjoyed a reclusive existence and spent time on her photography.

The family's beloved house became a curiosity because it looked like a jungle with a little path through the foliage and an array of cats and dogs. Only once in a while would you see Winnie. She'd pull back the curtains ever so slightly and demurely peek out, said Dayton. She had several yipping dogs who became especially startled at a child on a bicycle.

Winnie was the beloved heroine of Dade City's own version of Miss Havisham from Charles Dickens's *Great Expectations*. Like Miss Havisham, who was jilted at the altar and retreated from life, Winnie longed for normalcy and her very own family. Misunderstood, she retreated, and unfortunately, her reclusive status became the fodder of haunted suspicion.

For two decades, Winnie published extraordinary poems in the *Tampa Tribune*. She wrote comforting pieces for families whose loved ones were at war. She surely called on her own life experiences as she penned the most poignant of messages in the poetry. The following is an example from Sunday, February 29, 1948:

> BROTHERHOOD
> *If we could but feel that tie*
> *Of brotherhood…man to man*
> *And friend to friend*
> *Then prejudice and bigotry*
> *Would end; and by and by*
> *We'd have a world of happiness*

Built on God's plan
No selfishness to bring
On wars…instead there'd be
An honest way to settle
All debate; and we would see
More clearly everything
That now is dimmed by hate
Hate, bigotry and greed…
These three cause only sorrow.
And yet we find no way
By word or deed
To bring a happier tomorrow,
Must we go on forever more
With wars and strife?
Would not a way of kindness
And of brotherhood
Bring truer life?
—*Winifred Bridge Latham*

The White House at 12900 Fort King Road Keeps Mum About Peculiar History

"Hundreds of people have visited my house near AdventHealth Dade City [formerly Florida Hospital Dade City], and I am sometimes reminded of the both flamboyant and charming nature of its many lives," said Jeff Jeter. His grandfather imparted the diverse history of the house to Jeff. It was built by Emmett Evans in 1941 at what is now the apex of the bypass where it exits to Highway 301 north of Dade City by the old Pasco Packing Plant. It served as a tavern on the first floor and what Jeff described as an hourly hotel on the second.

Around 1952, Jeter said the house was moved across town to Fort King Highway—not an easy feat for a three-story structure to traverse power poles, intersections and the like.

Jeter described the house he inherited as an unusual frame house built of pine that has settled in its over eighty-year history. Built with an air space underneath, it attracted a good many curious racoons and other animals and has its share of creaks and settling noises. Several of the renters over time claimed it was haunted, and a few were eager to leave out of fright.

A few years ago, Jeff's mother opened a successful kindergarten and daycare called School Unique in the house. The school met with great success. The idea of a brothel converting to a charming daycare center was fascinating.

The three-story house had an outdoor stairway that was removed. It has been altered with siding and various coats of paint. A bullet hole under a rug in the living room hints at the former brothel's rugged past as a tavern/brothel. The experience of the Jeter haunted house is best described by the poem Jeter penned for St. Leo University's *Sandhill Review* a few years back.

> WHERE I LIVE BY JEFF JETER, III
> *Removed from the nurses, east of Fort King,*
> *Our lopsided hand-me-down stands.*
> *Once a small tavern with rooms by the hour,*
> *Her knobs have held hundreds of hands.*
> *Ripped from foundations, straddling axles,*
> *Removed to the outskirts of town.*
> *Bisected, dissected, annexed and sided,*
> *Warped the right places somehow.*
> *Grandparents rented upstairs apartments,*
> *Decades to teachers and entrepreneurs,*
> *Others young mothers, meth addicts.*
> *Often at night when I'm working alone,*
> *Jane, Isaac and Tanner in bed,*
> *I hear the odd footstep mounting the stair,*
> *But figure it's all in my head.*

UNCLE JESSE ROBERTS SUGGESTS SINGING TO A BEAR AIN'T GONNA TURN OUT WELL

Jesse Frances Roberts pounded brass (vernacular for telegraph operator) and was the first railway agent in Dade City, arriving in 1882 when supplies came via oxen cart from Ocala to Tampa. He oversaw the old narrow-gauge rails that were placed three feet apart. (Remnants of many narrow-gauge tracks abound in rural Pasco.) The South Florida Railroad was opened in 1887 from Pemberton's Ferry (Croom) to Lakeland. A consummate storyteller,

State Archives of Florida.

Roberts related the trafficking of produce loads that came from the modern tracks, which were squeezed onto the narrow-gauge tracks. The produce wobbled back and forth as the small engine attempted to maneuver the heavy loads, "never more than three cars." Many serious accidents occurred in the attempted use of the narrow-gauge tracks, which were more commonly used for the turpentine industry.

A favorite frightening story about the energetic Mr. Roberts was reported in the *Dade City Banner* in 1923 about an 1882 Sunday afternoon escapade. Churchgoing was the norm for everyone, and if you didn't show up for the Sunday service, neighbors came calling to see if you were ailing. As Roberts was leaving the Baptist church (which was then located at the site of the Dade City Cemetery), his trusty dog, Rascal, was waiting by the church door to accompany him home, and before Roberts could begin his journey, Rascal dashed off in a spectacle of barking and commotion. Folks scattered in fear. Rascal had caught scent of a bear. Uncle Jesse and Rascal, along with Jim Grady (later a Pasco sheriff), chased the bear through the hammocks until two o'clock the next morning, nearly seventeen hours. Uncle Jesse said he subscribed to the religious practice of the day of "not working on Sunday," and he reckoned they never hunted down that bear because of the botch of tailing him on a Sunday. The bear, however, was ultimately too friendly with people for his own good and the safety of pioneers, and he met his destiny at the homestead of Bob Sumner a few days later. "Too bad the bear liked our Sunday singing; didn't turn out too well for him though!" quipped Uncle Jesse.

Mysterious Brown House of River Road

The cypress homestead of Ashley McMillian and Elizabeth Sumner McMillian rests on River Road. Their homestead application with then-president Grover Cleveland was dated November 14, 1888. Unfortunately, Ashley died from appendicitis in the house in 1892. His wife, Elizabeth, lived until 1918.

In its over 130 years, the house has undoubtedly stood proudly through many changes. People refer to it as the Brown House, likely because of the unpainted cypress, but it was actually built or early owned by a family with the surname of Brown, explained Susan McMillian, a descendant.

As renovations were being completed on the interior, the owner experienced several anomalies. As she was beginning to paint, the ghostly resident seemed to dislike the painting, and items were mysteriously displaced. The owner, Sheryl Bryant, finally declared that she would continue painting until done and preferred not to be interrupted. Also, it is common to hear pots and pans rattling or noises in the bedroom.

Left: Brown House served as the homestead of Ashley McMillian and Elizabeth Sumner McMillian on River Road. *Billy Grant.*

Below: Filming of 1900s-era six-part series titled *Preach* on River Road at the Brown House. *Billy Grant.*

The house was selected by NFocus Media Production (Tim Register as producer/director, Lakeland, Florida) for consideration in a miniseries depicting the 1900s, with a prospective title of *Preach*. For the movie set, the cracker-style house was surrounded by horse and buggy, people in period clothing and cars from the Model T era.

Mount Zion Cemetery

Ronnie Collins, lifelong resident of Dade City, related in an interview that he and his two friends had a surreal experience at Mount Zion Cemetery in 1964. "It was just not too long after our graduation from high school. We were three teenagers who had rented a house in San Antonio, Florida, and we were enjoying the newfound freedom and responsibilities. Driving around on a Saturday night, we ended up at Zion Cemetery at Mount Zion Road. The three of us dared each other to walk through the cemetery for whatever reason, but we were kids. It was a really dark night."

Ronnie reported that it did not take long for the three of them to hightail it back to their car and their rented bachelor pad house. "There above the many cemetery markers in the 1871 cemetery that serves as the resting place for the remains of over 1,200 memorials were what appeared to be tiny lights…illumination [orbs]. We had never seen anything like it," he said.

"Some three weeks later, also on a weekend evening, two girls drove up to our house and inquired if we three fellows had ever been to Mount Zion Cemetery at night. We just stared at the girls, wondering if this was a weird coincidence. Then they warned us to never go to that cemetery at night because we would see unexplained phantom lights."

He was very clear that the half a dozen or so marble-size floating green lights were unique and unexplainable. Now mature adults, one of the three teenage boys has passed away and another has spent his life working for the Pasco Parks Department. Asked if they talked about their scary experience since, Ronnie responded that they had not dwelled on the experience, as the reactions were strong.

Ronnie added, "You may believe it or not, but it happened and not only the green lights but the random warning from the unknown girls put us on high alert about the Mount Zion Cemetery. No, we never went back."

The history of the Mount Zion Cemetery and the Fort Dade Methodist Church is of Pasco pioneer settlers. A historic marker reads, "Mt. Zion Methodist Church was organized in 1871. A two-story structure built of hand-hewn timbers and sawed rough boards on land donated by Nathan A. Carter—with the second floor reserved for the Masonic Lodge—was completed in 1872 when the first burial was made. The building was destroyed by a hurricane October 25, 1921."

Dr. William Wallace Cochran had a unique burial in 1889. He left instructions to be buried with his feet to the south. Bill Cochran, his great-grandson, said, "All I know is that he chose to have his feet to the south so

Mount Zion Cemetery. *Ernest E. Wise.*

on Resurrection Day he would rise facing south," rather than the traditional east, as a final statement of his support of the Confederacy.

Perhaps not the only non-reconstructed southerner, another local, William Green, reported seeing faint ghostly figures of gray uniformed soldiers marching across the road one foggy morning while driving by the cemetery.

A plaque at the cemetery is tucked in among majestic oaks and draped with Spanish moss. It reads, "In Loving Memory of the Pioneer Families of Pasco County."

3
Shroud of Misfortune on Lake Pasadena

Inhabitants occupied Lake Pasadena dating to 10,000 BCE. An interpretation of this village's history leads one to ask what might have been as it navigated calamity over time. The unknown but preeminent occupants predate Europeans by eons, as they migrated to Florida during the last ice age.

Ghost stories are pervasive on sacred Indian grounds. Phantom noises and a foggy consciousness of haunted space abound. The guesswork of folklore presumes that such grounds are not possessed by the spirits of these hunters and gatherers but are protected by the spirits that stand sentinel over the sacred grounds. So, how do we know Lake Pasadena is such a place? Lake Pasadena, situated between Zephyrhills, Wesley Chapel and Dade City, was an Indian settlement thousands of years ago.

James Thorner, in his *Times* article on February 24, 2004, titled "On the Trail of Ancient People," wrote, "Outcrops of flint-like coral rock from ancient seas that once covered Pasco were a perfect material for stone age tools. Neighborhoods such as Citrus Trace, Fox Ridge, Stagecoach, and Wesley Chapel were built atop hunting camps where hunter-gatherers chipped coral rock tools 3,000 to 7,000 years ago and left their scraps behind."

The treasure-trove of artifacts found particularly in the Lake Pasadena area gives a hazy glimpse at its past. Frank Hoff, a well-known collector said, "They [collectors] want to avoid the fate of Lake Pasadena," explaining that parts of it have been ravished by collectors who call it pothole city.

Lake Pasadena holds onto a treasure-trove of Native American secrets. *J. Thomas Touchton.*

Barry Wharton, a Tampa historian, said it looks like it "was nailed by a Munchkin bombing raid, as looters have dug there for decades." Hedman reported in a 2003 article that artifacts have been found in the area to indicate nomadic people came before to make tools from the outcroppings of agate coral that was prevalent then. This manufacturing site covered several square miles at the south and southwest part of what is now Lake Pasadena.

While Thorner shared that thousands of suburban Pasco families slumber atop buried history, Lake Pasadena, with the abundant water supply and rich vegetation, was a favored area, and the treasure-trove of lithics attests to that, although we do not have names or details of their owner and users' humanity. We can only imagine.

The first officially documented residents, however, were the Eufala Seminoles in the village of Toadchudka in the 1780s. They migrated from Alabama around 1767 and later established Etowahchutka, which was deserted in 1836 because of the Second Seminole War.

Early settlement history encompasses the settlement of Prospect and Lake Buddy, which evolved into Lake Pasadena by the 1880s. Williams Cemetery is the resting place of many of the pioneers, and a story of doom haunts the origin of the cemetery and personifies the frantic tug-of-war between Native Americans and early settlers. Perhaps part legend, the tale unfolds that the Williams family allowed a caravan of settlers to camp on their hillside, as they were off on an excursion for supplies, which meant being absent for a few days. To their horror, the Williams family found that the party had been annihilated, presumably by a Native American band. They buried the battered corpses in a mass grave, which was to become part of Williams Cemetery.

Orange fever had emerged around 1873, and Lake Pasadena was ideal "for the picking." In 1885, a forty-acre tract with a log house and 150 orange trees sold for $750, said Hedman. With the coming of the railroad soon after, produce could be shipped to the northern markets. The sheer beauty of the magnificent lake and the rolling hills, now dotted with lush citrus, appealed to rich northerners, and Lake Pasadena became known for a short time as the English colony.

Two hotels, both built by Alfred and Anna Drew, were the Pasadena Hotel near the railroad and the Lake View Highlands Hotel located near Pasadena and Chesterfield Roads, just off Clinton Avenue. The Lake View was a luxury hotel that catered to Bostonians. Aston F. Embry wrote in a 1957 letter about his first job as a fifteen-year-old at Lake View:

> *The massive hotel stood overlooking Lake Pasadena. It was painted white with touches of green and yellow…roses trellised against the front verandas. Women promenaded the veranda with their long dresses dragging the floor, making Embry's porch-sweeping job a lot easier.*
>
> *A tennis court, bowling green and club building were also included on the ten-acre hotel grounds. A boardwalk extended the length of the rounds, ending at a dock where rowboats waited for fishermen.*
>
> *Embry's job also included helping those fishermen guests. "I was often the oarsman—and probably a rather unreliable one—while the Yanks did the fishing," he wrote.*
>
> *And times were good in the upscale Pasadena community for some five years as citrus continued to bring in money to residents, as tourists flocked to the area.*

The opulence of the era spawned an overconfident certainty of Lake Pasadena's magnitude of status in the county that was then Hernando, but the year 1889 would change the trajectory of the path of the thriving village. The triumph of Dade City as the county seat from the election of 1889 sealed a kind of fate that would allow Dade City to withstand hard times ahead that would doom Lake Pasadena to anonymity.

First came the devastating freeze of December 29, 1894, in which young citrus trees were killed and unpicked fruit destroyed. There was a glimmer of hope as the invasive frost was late in the season, but then came the second freezing night of February 7, 1895, which sealed the fate. Guests at the Lake View were said to have literally left the opulent dining area to take a surrey to the train station to stay overnight at the smaller hotel near the train station to find passage back to Boston.

Then, in 1901, just as the proprietor, Charles Ramsdell, was planning an elegant New Year's Day rebirth of the luxurious hotel, a fire erupted. Guests in their night shirts and gowns frantically escaped to the grounds to watch the hotel burning to the ground. Ramsdell had every room booked for the winter season, and the Dade City elite had been invited to attend the grand opening for New Year's Day 1902. The fireworks of that New Year's Eve (theorized to have started from an unattended stove fire) sealed the final fate for Lake Pasadena in a kind of *Titanic* manner, compounded by the fact that the hotel was insured for only one-fourth of its value, making the prospect of rebuilding very dim.

Although plans for the area to reemerge as a resort were in the works at the time of great prosperity in 1924, when Alfred Brown announced plans for a four-hundred-room hotel on LeHeup Hill overlooking Pasadena, the arrival of the land boom plummeted the concept.

To uncover the history of Lake Pasadena today, one can travel to nearby Dade City, as significant buildings were physically relocated from the lake community. The 1892 Anglican church building was moved by mules to Dade City in 1902 to be used as the St. Mary's Episcopal Church building, and the 1885 Lake Pasadena schoolhouse was redeployed to Church Avenue in 1910 to serve as the Bethel Primitive Baptist Church.

As with the demise of the elegant hotels, the stylish houses that had dotted Lake Pasadena were largely destroyed by forest fires that came from cattle ranchers burning off the wooded acres of pastureland. Very few houses remain that tell the story.

It is possible to track down some of the older homes. Joy Lynn has lived in a home that was built in 1932 by Wendell LeHeup, whose father, William Alfred LeHeup, homesteaded in the area in 1911. She serves as director of the Dade City Heritage and Cultural Museum and said, "You can fill an entire book on the haunted history of Lake Pasadena." She offers walking tours and a look at photographs and belongings of people. "Each time people come in, we have another story to tell them."

Fordyce house in Lake Pasadena. *Author's collection.*

Another home that is revered is known as the Dew house and was built in 1913 by William Dew, Howard McKillips and Charlie Knapp. Heart pine lumber was milled at Greer's mill, and it debuted a three-fireplace chimney.

In addition, the Fordyce home is described in the venerable local history book *The Historic Places of Pasco County* by James J. Horgan, Alice F. Hall and Edward J. Herrmann. They state, "The distinctive original features are still intact, notably the turret and the wraparound porch. Owned by the Fordyce family, it is the only remaining home in this neighborhood from the turn-of-the-century period when the Lake View Highlands Hotel was a prominent resort on Lake Pasadena."

Owner Barbara Berger denied any mysterious activity in the time she has occupied the home, although Hedman described in a *Tribune* article in 2003 that a house guest witnessed a doorknob moving on its own accord and cold bursts, while Dayton similarly recounted that Glidewell had told him of a doorknob turning with nobody on the other side, which frightened "a man who was not easily startled." For a grand old house of over 130 years, it might be explained by walls out of plumb or any host of other aging infirmities.

Buried Treasure on Hen-Cart Road

According to Carl Taylor, hidden treasure was buried around 1840 at Williams Hammock on what is now Handcart Road. A small party of soldiers accompanied the army paymaster to Fort Brooke (Tampa), guarding money intended to pay the garrison. For an unknown reason, they marched along what was then known as Hen-Cart Road rather than the Fort King Military Road—perhaps they feared an attack. As they camped at the hammock, they got word that a war party was coming. The paymaster buried the loot at the foot of a distinctive leaning tree in the hammock and placed a copper kettle over the leather saddlebag. Said to be a fortune in Spanish doubloons, it has not yet been located.

One might say the spirits of Native Americans have influenced a series of bad luck that has befallen the community, yet a visit to the Pasadena Fish Camp, coined a bass fisherman's delight for well over fifty years, may indicate all the Natives, past and present, are smiling.

4
DARBY AND BRADLEY MASSACRE SITE SITS ON AMUSEMENT PARK

Perhaps best known for two unique and diverse peculiarities in history, this little agrarian berg was named for John W. Darby, who lived from 1832 to 1894. A farming community with majestic oaks and cypress persisted because of open range. It was resplendent with cracker cattle, horses and feral hogs, not to mention timber and turpentine. Two prominent pieces of notoriety include the Bradley Massacre (also known as the Darby Massacre) and the worldwide fame of country music duo the Bellamy Brothers, who graduated from nearby Pasco High School and participate in the Tampa Bay community as volunteers and proud preservers of Florida cracker history.

"There's a lot of old Bellamy spirits wandering around there. We were raised there, grew up there, and I can't imagine ever living anywhere else," said Howard Bellamy in 2002.

Native Floridian Howard Bellamy shared some insights into Darby, which houses the family's generational ranch.

> Our native cattle are what the Spanish brought in and the family would cross the cracker cattle with the brahma cattle and they could endure anything and withstand all the elements. We were called cattle hunters not cowboys, because you had to have a tracking dog and the cattle would hide. It was a different lifestyle then. It made for an interesting time. Our dad played dobro [resonating guitar] and started us into music as we played and sang with him and his friends, but we are still very much ranchers at heart. "Never get too high or too low," my dad would always say, in regard to the humility of the people in Darby.

Bradley Massacre

One does not discuss Florida frontier history without mentioning the Bradley Massacre. The preeminent historical fabric of Darby emerges from accounts of the massacre at the homestead of Captain Robert Duke Bradley.

The date was May 14, 1856, and Bradley lay bedridden. The tragedy may have been revenge. Captain Bradley surrendered his military commission due to malaria after accomplished involvement in the Second Seminole War, where, among other feats, he hunted down Nethlockemathlar, the brother of Tiger Tail (Thlocko Tustenuggee), who was a strategic chief.

Nonetheless, late in the day on May 14, Bradley heard the undeniable sounds of a war party. His precious eleven-year-old, Mary Jane Bradley, was shot through the heart. (Sam Cloud's account in the *Peninsular Gazette* gives a vivid account in which Bradley commanded Mary Jane to lie down, but in the fear of the moment, she ran to her mother, who was in the cooking area of the cabin, which had not been completed. Through a hole in the unfinished chimney, she was shot and died instantly.) Her fifteen-year-old

Painting by Clinton Inman, completed February 2020, of an interpretation of the Bradley Massacre, which occurred in Darby, Florida.

brother, William Brown Bradley, was then hit with two muskets. Having his father's fortitude, William struggled into the cabin and grabbed his rifle, firing before he collapsed in death as well.

Since 2014, a seasonal attraction at the location of the massacre (now 27839 St. Joe Road) known as Scream-A-Geddon, has received countless visitors. Actors and visitors report seeing two shadowy figures hovering near a pond. Conjecture is that the shadowy figures are the ghosts of Mary Jane and William Bradley, whose young lives were abruptly cut short, or perhaps warriors who were marched away to Oklahoma in the Trail of Tears in the months that followed.

Historians believe remnants of the Bradley homestead may be pinpointed to the amusement park site in a low-lying area, perhaps a pond, because research has revealed the vicinity was extremely drought-ridden for several years prior to the attack.

5
LAND O'LAKES

FROM STAGECOACH TO EDWARD SCISSORHANDS

From anonymity to tremendous growth, central Pasco has evolved from timber and turpentine to suburban settlement. The old maps make no mention of the name Land O'Lakes. "The area lacks written history," wrote Marilyn Kalfus in 1978. In 1927, Carl H. Rerick wrote in the *Banner*, "Numerous lakes dot the landscape so that nearly every resident has a lake or shares one with a neighbor."

The Seminoles populated the area until the late nineteenth century, so settlement was riskier and challenging for pioneers coming to take advantage of land opportunities. The essence of Native American heritage still permeates the community.

Major Bradley was one of the few homesteaders from the Armed Occupation Act in what was the Land O'Lakes area before he relocated to Darby. Various tiny communities developed in the vicinity that were spawned from lumbering and turpentine stills along the railroad. They were Big Cypress, Disston, Drexel, Ehren, Fivay Junction, Mexico, Myrtle-Denham, Pleasant Hills, Shingleton, Stemper and Tucker.

The name came into existence by popular vote on June 13, 1949, at a meeting called by the Denham-Drexel Civic Association. Differing opinions on the origin of the name exist; one theory is that it came from the Minneapolis-based Land O'Lakes butter company, and the more sophisticated explanation is that it suited the composite of lakes in the area. It incorporated two main settlements, Drexel and Myrtle-Denham. Some old-timers say that Ehren, a community three miles to the west, was also included.

It is difficult to write about the area without mention of the stagecoach road. Stagecoaches played a vital role before railroads. One of the oldest lines started in the 1840s, was discontinued during the Civil War and ceased by 1907.

The mighty Concord Stage Line stopped at Fort Taylor, just south of the county line, before stopping at Ehren. It followed a trail known as the Twenty-Mile Level Road (as it was twenty miles from Tampa) and was a mainstay of transportation and delivery of goods until the railroads arrived around 1890. The sand road connected Tampa to Brooksville, Ocala, Palatka and Gainesville and went through the center of Pasco, meandering to Myrtle Post Office and then north Brooksville. The Twenty-Six-Mile house was the relay station where you could get fresh horses. The first post office came to Myrtle-Denham in 1893. Its first postmaster, William Whitfield, a corageous military man, served for about twenty-one years and unfortunately died after being bitten by a mad dog.

All of the communities were sawmill towns. The mills either burned to the ground or ceased by the time of the Great Depression.

William Kersey helped to build U.S. 41, which was built "by hand and mules." He also helped build Ten-Cent Road. Although some believed the name of the road derived from a charge that Indians collected to travel on it, longtime Land O'Lakes resident and former county tax appraiser Ted Williams explained, "They had cut cross ties and there was more timber on one side than on the other so there was a ten-cent variance in the cost."

By 1978, the area was beginning to emerge. Loren Woreley, developer of Foxwood, said, "It was hot as a pistol for people." Other subdivisions at that time included Lake Padgett Estates and Turtle Lake.

Walking the Stagecoach Trail Alone, James Dixon Met His Fate

Dixon's Hill near Ehren cutoff holds ominous history that haunted the storyteller. Taylor chronicled the ghastly account of 1853 in which a weary traveler and prospector, James Dixon, met his demise while walking to Tampa. Allen O. Pearce, an early surveyor in Ehren and the nearby area that would later be named Land O'Lakes, related the story with vivid detail, as it was the kind of story to conjure vivid images that would creep into your thoughts on sleepless nights and give you a start.

In the area where the old stagecoach route meandered between Brooksville and Tampa, there was a place known as Dixon Hill. It was an assembling place for cow hunters engaged in roundups. James Dixon was walking on foot by himself, following the stagecoach road between Fort Taylor—located near the current line between Hernando and Pasco Counties—and heading toward Tampa. As dusk fell, he stopped for the night at the homestead of Bill Whitfield. The next morning, he again set out on the stagecoach road toward Tampa.

Carl B. Taylor wrote in his 1927 account in the *Tampa Sunday Tribune*, "Dixon was never seen alive again, but his fate can be deduced by circumstantial evidence that is too conclusive to be disputed." They discovered a kind of survival of the fittest crime scene. Taylor continued:

> *Evidently Dixon turned aside from the road, which was simply a pair of wheel ruts through the sand, when he reached the hill and sat under a tree to rest. He had walked many miles and was hot and tired and evidently fell asleep. While sleeping, a panther, of which there were many in those days, attacked and killed him, and then, having satisfied its appetite, dragged his body into a lake at the foot of the hill and left it.*
>
> *The tragedy was discovered a day or two later when Allen's father, Samuel Jonathan Pearce in company with Henry Hancock, John Mizzell, and John McNatt, Sr., who were returning from a trip to Tampa, stopped to camp on the hill. They found Dixon's valise, saw the tracks of the panther, and the signs of the struggle, and following the trail made by dragging the body, discovered the corpse submerged in the muddy bottom of the pond.*
>
> *They were unable to recover Dixon's body but returned his valise to the family in Jacksonville along with an account of what had occurred. Pearce distinctly remembers the details of the account from his childhood, and related that since that tragedy, the hill was known as Dixon's Hill.*

"Dixon's Hill," added Pearce, "is located at the center of Section 9, Township 25, Range 19, and is in the geographical center of Pasco County. At the time the county was formed, the Aripeka Sawmills, owners of this property, offered it to the county as a site for the courthouse and county seat."

For many years after, the area was known as Dixon's Hill, but by 2020, the name had faded into obscurity. The wild ferocity of the endangered Florida panther remains, however, and take note that they are most active at night.

The abandoned Dupree Garden ruins in the Land O'Lakes vicinity stand as a ghostly remembrance of a spectacular botanical garden and attraction that opened at an inopportune time in history, 1940, by James Dupree. Elegant in its day with glass-bottomed boats and exhibits graced with smiling, gowned ladies color-coordinated with vibrant foliage, it closed by 1954. Residences now occupy the vast acreage, with the exception of the original limestone ticket booth, which holds the history as well as some crumbling limestone pillars. Recently, a curious guest stopped by to take a look. She related that it was "eerily silent, the decaying carcass of a deer lay to the south. There was a feeling of being watched somehow—bad juju, so we left quickly," adding that it must have been beautiful in its day.

Pasco's Frankenstein at Carpenter's Run in Central Pasco

Edward Scissorhands

In a new take on *Frankenstein*, the Land O'Lakes area helped to create a cutting-edge fairy tale in which Edward Scissorhands unwittingly fashions a suburban nightmare. When 20th Century Studios and Tim Burton, one of Hollywood's hottest leading film directors, with credits such as *Beetlejuice* and *Batman*, came scouting for a movie location for a horror film in 1990, there was speculation that it might be the beginning of a movie oasis for east and central Pasco County, especially as a spinoff from the opening of Disney MGM and Universal Studios in Orlando. The movie accountant, Jay Sedrish, even estimated it would bring $4 million into the local economy.

Pasco's own benevolent cross between Frankenstein's monster and Pinocchio provides a thought-provoking story with famed horror film actor Vincent Price as the father figure who designs a human played by Johnny Depp. Price's character dies before finalizing the masterpiece, and Scissorhands proceeds to awkwardly interact with suburbia and is accepted, rejected, scorned and appreciated. Making the best of what he has, he becomes proficient at crafting topiaries, cutting hair and sculpting ice creations.

Director Tim Burton found the suburban look he desired at Tinsmith Circle at the Carpenter's Run development on State Road 54. Next, he set out to transform Carpenter's Run into a suburban fantasy. Critics raved that every Scissorhands scene exploded with eye-popping elements. The pop fable offered a parody on society's unwillingness to accept differences and embrace divergent abilities and thinking.

The castle set of Edward Scissorhands housed the metaphorical hand posturing to the sky. The sheriff's department provided security for the lengthy filming, and the community embraced the creepy story as businesses contributed set objects, shrubbery and even trash collection. *Ted Johnson.*

The castle set along County Road 41 outside of Dade City housed a huge castle façade with an array of topiaries. When security for the isolated set failed, off-duty deputies were recruited from Jim Gillum's sheriff department. Ted Johnson was one of those deputies and had an opportunity to observe filming. He guarded Johnny Depp, Winona Ryder and several others, who he found to be engaging and easy to work with. Ted recalled some anecdotes—Depp in a tight-fitting, black leather costume suffering excruciating heat in the Florida sun and the innovative lightweight balsa wood polished to perfection used for the mock scissor hands. He recalled that the castle had a Hansel and Gretel look and reminisced about the crafted windows, which were purchased by local Jane Futch after the filming.

Leslie Gilmore-Lagosky was the catering manager at Saddlebrook Golf & Tennis Resort and became acquainted with the nearly one hundred actors and staff who were housed at the resort for several months during the filming. Danny Ondrejko, greens foreman for the movie, allowed her to photograph the set and explained some of the intricacies of the space. Leslie, quite the amateur photographer, shared her photographs in the community and even

Ted Johnson, an off-duty sheriff's officer, guarded Tim Burton and Johnny Depp in the filming of *Edward Scissorhands*. These interesting fairytale-like windows were purchased from the set by local citizen Jane Futch and were later sold in her estate sale. *Ted Johnson.*

Serving as the 1990s site of the filming of Pasco's cross between Frankenstein and Pinocchio, the area was transformed into an eerie site. The photographer and catering manager even won first prize at the county fair with her photo of the spooky castle. *Leslie Gilmore-Lagosky.*

Master greensman Danny Ondrejko cared for the plants on the set of *Edward Scissorhands*—a challenge, as the script called for before-and-after photos in regard to the metaphors of health and pain. *Leslie Gilmore-Lagosky.*

won first prize at the Pasco County Fair in 1991 for one of them. Brian Swann remembered visiting the set to drop off one of the extras. While waiting, he met actress Conchata Ferrell, who played Helen. He recalled that Ferrell had an exaggerated beehive hairdo as one of Scissorhands's designs, and he remembered the businesslike, focused atmosphere of the movie set.

Hal Lipper wrote in a 1990 *Times* piece, "There is a wondrous quality to *Edward Scissorhands* that is unlike any other movie….A marvelous social satire that revels in suburbia, it is a mystery tour; a parable so simple and seminal, it has no precedents. With his tangled black hair, leather bound torso and awkward, uncomfortable gestures, he is the physical embodiment of writer director, Tim Burton. His eyes silently beg, 'Accept me as I am and I'll take you to worlds you never knew existed,' Edward Scissorhands does exactly that."

With numerous Pasco extras in the movie, suspense mounted for the anticipated opening of the movie. The local theaters had celebrations, and a group of the folks from Carpenter's Run attended the showing at University Square Cinema. Steve McQuilkin reported in a December 14, 1990 *Tribune* piece, "Their reward came at the tail end of the credits when Burton thanked the residents of Carpenter's Run…especially those living in Tinsmith Circle where most of the movie was filmed. The residents whooped and clapped."

6
ODESSA AND THE JUSTICE OF SHERIFF BART

Odessa is on the border of Hillsborough and Pasco Counties and has a rugged history. It is perhaps one of the most vigilante of the settlements that sprouted. Between 1917 and 1918, in an era of eye-for-an-eye independence, eighteen men were killed in fights and only a few were investigated. The town was named by Peter Demens, a Russian developer of the Orange Belt Railway in 1888. Initially, a turpentine still and sawmill were operated by prisoners from a stockage just south of the county line. Soon after the turn of the century, Gulf Pine Lumber Company, which was sold to Dowling Lumber Company, and Lyon Lumber Company were in place. The mill owners built wood shanties for workers who lived brutal, subsistence lives of deprivation.

Like in a feudal system, the workers were paid in tokens that were redeemable at the commissaries. The average wage was a dollar a day for an eleven-hour day. By 1909, there were three hundred lumber men living in Odessa, and by 1918, at the height of the lumber industry, the town had two thousand residents, of whom twelve hundred worked in lumber and turpentine.

Life was unforgiving, and Odessa had a reputation for ruthless, hardworking and hard-drinking men. The legend of a particular incident is retold in the town and has taken on a life of its own.

Enter Sheriff Bartow Daniel Sturkie, regularly referred to as Bart. Sheriffs were powerful in that time and were known for autonomy that came down from the tradition of English common law but required snap timing and

Rugged Odessa. *State Archives of Florida.*

decisiveness. Bart, a native Alabamian, had strong opinions and relied on brute dumb luck. Many said he was guided by the spirit of the frontier.

In 1915, Sheriff Bart killed a person in a gunfight on Main Street in Odessa. Some thirty-three miles from the location, Bart was summoned for help by telephone on a Sunday, and subsequently, Bart and his deputy, H.E. Whitfield, arrived by train. The *Banner* stated, "Upon arriving at Odessa, the sheriff located Will Hyatt at his home and tried to place him under arrest. Hyatt resisted and, in the scuffle, which ensued, shot at the sheriff six times."

Dayton said Hyatt was drunk and did kill a mule and a dog. The *Dade City Banner* also mentioned, "Hyatt was searching for his wife and went about town shooting into windows and entering houses with the occupants fleeing before him while he emptied his pistol into walls and broke several windows. He also shot some chickens in the neighbors' yards and generally terrorized the town." In the aftermath, an investigation of the case was held in Judge Wilson's office, where the sheriff was cleared.

The body of Hyatt was buried at Odessa the following day. He left a young wife and a five-year-old daughter. The other lasting impression was on Bart, who was said to never carry a gun thereafter in the pursuit of his job. In the final year of his sheriff's reign, Bart revealed that he was haunted not only by the "gunfight in the Main Street of Odessa" but also by the other killings he was forced to accomplish. This weighed heavily on his conscience and troubled him immensely. As an executioner, protector and gunslinging powerhouse, he knew firsthand the suffering of others—he saw it up close and personal. Sheriff Bart had a kind of aura, and tales were spun of his legendary prowess. "He was the kind of person who could stop a fight by walking into a room," Dayton said. "He was a big man."

"Even after the shootout, knife fights happened nightly and gunfights usually at least once a week in Odessa. The commissary was the hub of activity as many mill workers were escaped convicts from north Florida and Georgia," said Hedman in a 2002 *Tribune* article titled "Former Timber Town of Odessa Keeps an Eye to the Past."

The lumber resources were depleted in the 1920s, and Odessa attempted to rebuild its identity. In 1925, the community was celebrating an anticipated Cinderella event, as Belasco Productions had chosen Odessa for a $250,000 movie studio that would revolutionize the area, but within months, the real estate boom began to turn, and Belasco pulled out of its endeavor. On January 21, 1937, at 8:15 a.m. half a mile west of Odessa, Atlantic Coast Line had a devastating train crash in which five Pullman cars headed toward St. Petersburg were flung off the tracks. There were numerous injuries, especially to the Black waiter, who was hurled against the wall of the car while serving breakfast. Investigation showed a rail had been jutted out to the side. Perhaps it was foul play, but nothing was ever proven.

Sheriff Bart Sturkie served from 1904 to 1916 and 1920 to 1924. *Mary Powell Ward.*

Sheriff Bart, however, had a remarkable career that might be compared to Wyatt Earp and others of the Wild West. In office during Prohibition, Bart's dose of self-proclaimed law enforcement sovereignty was heightened. Dayton revealed that the sheriff would enforce Prohibition and posture going after the moonshiners and blind tigers, as they were called, who produced or served forbidden alcohol, but loathed the ardent Prohibitionists because he thought it was stupid. Over the course of his career as sheriff, for four terms from 1904 to 1916 and again from 1920 to

1924, after serving as a Dade City marshal for four terms, he maintained a tight grip on the area and was known to look the other way when he thought it best.

A few snippets of his career give an idea of Bart:

- In 1907, the *Weekly Tribune* said Sheriff Bart was searching around for blind tigers.
- In July 1909, when Preston Gillett showed up at Bart's office to confess that he had gunned down Tom Ellis, Bart turned a blind eye and presented Gillett with two shotgun shells to reimburse him. An insidious feud had been going on for years between the Ellis and Gillett families, and in 1907, Tom Ellis was charged with homicide and fratricide. Each time, he managed to escape prosecution, only for the feud to continue with another murder.
- In 1909, Sheriff Bart slipped away silently to New Orleans in search of bond jumper Dr. J. Martin Posey, a well-known Hudson physician who jumped his whopping $2,000 bond. Bart said he traveled undercover because the doctor had thousands of friends in Florida who would help him out if they knew Bart was on his path. The doctor was upset at R.A. Ellis, the developer of Aripeka, who had impacted him financially with his development. Ellis bought a lot of land in the vicinity of Hudson, where Dr. Posey resided, and cut it up into lots for sale. Trying to dissuade development, the prestigious physician proclaimed the water on the lots was poisoned. When Ellis rebuked him as a downright liar, Dr. Posey packed his pistol and grabbed his shotgun and went in search of Mr. Ellis to defend his honor. An encounter ensued in which Ellis got the better of the argument. Dr. Posey responded by shooting Ellis with the pistol. Ellis came very near dying, and charges of assault with intent to murder in the first degree were sustained by the jury when the case went to trial despite the costly defense of Posey by Colonel Robert W. Davis. Sheriff Bart brought him back.
- Also in 1909, a bit sheepish about it, Bart went to Hillsborough County to pick up two jailbreakers, Wilson and Wood. The two had broken out of the jail in Dade City and wounded an officer after being apprehended in neighboring Hillsborough County. Bart took no chances with the men. He handcuffed them and chained them together and firmly informed the two fugitives,

within hearing distance of fellow officers, that he had a loaded .44 on each of his hips.

- In 1913, Bart carried out his sheriff duties by hanging Tom Bush for the murders of Annie Johnson and Hoyt Houston near Odessa. In March, Tom became vehemently jealous of Hoyt Houston, who he thought was giving too much attention to Annie Johnson, a gal with whom he was infatuated. He gunned down Annie and then Hoyt. This was not the only hanging that Bart facilitated in his years as sheriff.

   The *Times* reported, "A great crowd had gathered in and about the jail yard...and the scene presented almost a festive aspect. Bush was conducted up the steps of the scaffold to the trap by Bart and two deputies. He walked steadily...after he made a short talk and as he concluded, stood perfectly still while Bart placed two leather straps about his legs and cord over his suspended arms. The noose was adjusted about his neck and the cap placed over his head and the trap was spring. Bush fell six to eight feet, though his neck was not broken.... Twenty minutes later the physician declared him dead."

- In 1915, a prisoner was taken from the jailhouse, which also included the living quarters of Sheriff Bart and his family. (Dayton explained that a perk for living in the sheriff's quarters was that the sheriff's wife received a salary for cooking for the inmates.) Deputy Kirby, in his night shirt, was overtaken by a mob of approximately twenty masked men from nearby Trilby who put a shotgun under Kirby's chin, demanded he hand over the keys and then broke the lock and hauled out a Black prisoner named Will Leak. Leak was lynched in front of Hilliard's Barber Shop in the center of the town of Trilby and was found hanging from an oak tree the next morning. This was not Sheriff Bart's most legendary leadership, as the local newspaper reported that Bart was present in his quarters beside the jail and did not hear the commotion because he was sick. Dayton said city tradition was less charitable to him and insisted that Bart, a known tippler, was actually drunk and derelict of his duty. Nobody would dare confront him.

- "John O'Berry Is Foully Murdered," wrote the *Dade City Banner* on November 12, 1915, "in Trilby at the rear of the Bankston & Stephen's store." The murder was believed to have been over

a cattle dispute. O'Berry was in the store and stepped out of the back into the alley and was drilled by a ton of buckshot. Bart convened a coroner's jury, but they were unable to learn anything.
- Also in 1915, Bart had to contend with enormous crowds at the county courthouse when Ivey Overstreet was acquitted for killing Tom Scott, who was ambushed with Elmore Tucker of Richland as they were crossing the Withlacoochee River at Cow's Ford while his brothers, Taft and Preston Overstreet, were bound over to the grand jury. The first witness to the stand was Elmore Tucker, who had been wounded. He gave a detailed description of the shooting, identifying Taft and Preston Overstreet and another unknown person who was shooting from a hollow cypress tree. Another witness said that Ivey Overstreet had lost a cow in the vicinity of the Tuckers' home and claimed that if he ever saw them near his house, he would fill them full of buckshot.
- In 1916, Bart requested the bloodhounds be sent from Polk County so that he could track the retaliation killer of Tom Pierce, who had allegedly killed Adolphus Lewis at Fivay. The son of the Pasco County surveyor, Pierce was said to have killed Lewis because of some land dealings with the Aripeka Sawmill. At the bloody scene, Bart was infuriated as Pierce was shot twenty-five times from the front with No. 8 shot, which tore a huge hole in his lower back.
- In 1921, Bart had to arrest Mayor George J. Frese of San Antonio. Frese was operating a moonshine still on the second floor of his residence. Bart destroyed the still and kept some of the liquor as evidence.
- In 1922, a crowd of two thousand people was gathered at noon to attend the funeral services of J.W. Waters, the Prohibition agent who was slain with A.F. Crenshaw. Sheriff Bart marched six men to the county jail by a posse of officers that included a representation of the Thomas National Detective Agency and the chief general Prohibition agent of Tampa. "No troubles were experienced though they were prepared for a gun battle," stated the *Ocala Evening Newspaper* on October 7, 1922.
- Also in 1922, Bart was called to New Port Richey about a corpse that was found encased in fresh concrete. He was in regular communication with the chief of police in New York

City about the missing man. The *Times* reported on August 22, 1922, "Last Saturday a Mrs. Wesa was passing a Mr. Neaisinanen's house and looked through and saw a hat. She became suspicious and reported it to the justice of the peace."

- Later in December 1922, Bart was on the trail of the bank robbers who got away with $250 in cash at a stick-up at the Bank of Trilby.
- In 1923, Sheriff Bart offered a $100 reward for locating I.D. Harrington, who had escaped from jail.
- Also in 1923, Bart was on the trail of the payroll thief Charley Gerkin, who held up Cummer Cypress Mill in Lacoochee for the company's payroll. When the two were apprehended in Tampa, Bart went there and brought them back by train. "Bond or no bond, they are going back to Pasco County," said Bart.

7
Crystal Springs Fountain of Youth and Surviving Extinction

C rystal Springs has seen transformations and the abrupt extinction of resources and systems over time, making for a shaky, if not sometimes scary, past. Monstrous prehistoric animals, Native American hunters and gatherers, a socialist commune and weird food have impacted this extremly southeastern corner of Pasco County just above the Hillsborough County line. Wilfred T. Nell reported on the pioneer past in November 1979:

> *At the western outskirts of the Pasco County community, a large spring and half-a-dozen smaller ones arise from caverns in the underlying limestone. They form a single pool about 1,000 feet long. The Florida Geological Survey has several times measured this temperature, finding it to be 75 degrees. In very remote times, even before the coming of the Indians, sinkhole springs such as the one in East Pasco were waterholes where Ice Age animals came to drink or bathe and where sometimes they left their bones. Remarkably free of bacteria and dissolved oxygen, the bones and teeth of larger animals often did not decay. Crystal Springs has yielded the remains of a giant-ground-sloth, an armadillo-like beast, a dire-wolf and the mammoth elephant, among others.*

All nature of Native American artifacts has been found at the springs and the surrounding area, including flint spearpoints, flint chips and tools.

The unique, comparatively modern history of Crystal Springs (since 1907), originally named Jarve Springs, includes a socialist colony, belief that the ancient springs were a magical fountain of youth and a distinctive vegetable called the dasheen. Aside from the myth of a magical spring, the dispute over the distribution of the communally held land included a brutal murder that was disguised as an accident.

New-Age thinking at the turn of the century produced an idealistic group in Ruskin that lived and worked in a cooperative society. In 1911, Arthur B. Hawk formed an offshoot cooperative homestead company in Toledo, Ohio, known as the Common Good Society and purchased some twenty-four thousand acres. Similar to neighboring Zephyrhills, the area was attractive to veterans of the Grand Army of the Republic, and Hawk's innovative approach to advertising was affective. He offered small parcels of land for the "average man" to acquire a farm in the ideally warm climate of Central Florida. Added to this was the appeal to have perpetual access to the springs, which were said to be a fountain of health. The magical, pristine springs provided healing, and some reports said that the lobby of the local hotel was filled with discarded crutches and canes that were thrown aside by folks who swam in the waters of Crystal Springs and received the miracle cure.

Common Good Society Hall in 1915. *State Archives of Florida.*

The cooperative dictated that when one hundred families populated the society, control of their land would be signed over to them. Later on, the members of the Common Good Society were swindled out of their claims to the springs by Hawk, who sold them. Protests lasted for years, and it was theorized that Kenneth Burks was even killed over the ownership and pushed in front of a train on his way to New York while holding physical proof that the sale of the springs was illegal. Walking the Old Crystal Springs Cemetery, you'll see that many plots belong to pioneers of the innovative socialist agricultural community that ultimately failed.

The society built a community building for regular meetings and used it as a church. The residents wanted an honest-to-goodness church, and they had the idea to recruit John Nutting, who was then an octogenarian. The revered and highly popular hymn "Little Brown Church in the Vale" had been written by Dr. William S. Pitts from the church in Nashua, Iowa, that Reverend Nutting pastored. The Crystal Springs residents wanted to create their own unique version of the Little Brown Church that featured a tower to accommodate a band of several pieces designed by Nutting himself. It was dedicated in November 1914, and Nutting pastored there until his death. A flood in the 1920s devastated parts of the area, and the Little Brown Church became a chicken house; thus, the Little Brown Church met extinction as well.

8
PORT RICHEY'S SACRED GROUND

To visit Oelsner Mound (Eschasakotes) in Port Richey is to acknowledge the footprints of the first people who peered down from the highest point overlooking the industrious Native American village. A popular, recurring horror movie theme chronicles the ills that befall those who disturb the sanctity of sacred Indian burial grounds. In reality, however, mounds are covered by homes, shops, parking areas and roads we drive on throughout Pasco County. The few surviving ones are temple or ceremonial.

The Eschasakotes Mound personifies the antiquity of Port Richey. Climb the stairs and look around, and you can imagine the expansive village of the indigenous people of eons ago—so long ago it is difficult to measure. (Tribes date from the Weeden Island II period, 750 CE to 1000 CE, to the Safety Harbor period, 800 CE to European contact.)

The mound was first excavated by Sylvanus T. Walker in the spring of 1879. He created two reports: one describing the mounds he excavated and another reporting on shell heaps in the area. He found two mounds: a mound of residence and a second that revealed extensive human remains and artifacts.

Unlike Clarence B. Moore, who followed with a large crew in 1903, Walker mentioned hiring one or two men skilled at both snake catching and excavation. Frugality was essential to Walker on his humble excavation of the Pithlachascotee River area, and it cost a mere ten dollars. It is unfortunate that his research was not taken more seriously. In 1881, he described changes

Oelsner Mound in New Port Richey. *Author's collection.*

in artifacts evident at different levels and divided the mound into stages based on this data.

Moore's extensive diggings found 150 skeletal remains and gave him the opportunity to catalogue artifacts. Unfortunately, as was the practice in the time after his excavation, the mound was reconstructed. In 1924, John T. Hill sold the property housing the mounds (which remained unchanged since the reconstruction) to Rudolph Oelsner, thus the name given to the mound. A house had been erected in 1915 on the western side of the mound.

In 1953, archaeologists explored the mound once again. They noted that Oelsner had built stairs on the east side of the platform mound to provide easy access to the breathtaking view of the river, which had been the intent of the indigenous builders in the selection of the location. Another house was added on the eastern portion of the burial mound, destroying what the archaeologists had studied in 1953.

The mound property was owned by Martha Oelsner for fifty-seven years. She made a series of false claims about Native American culture, stating that remains of Calusa Indians were entombed there and lacking an understanding of the history. She left the mound to the Florida sheriff's Youth Ranch as part of her estate. With the tenacity of Alice Hall of Zephyrhills and Governor Bob Graham and a series of lengthy negotiations, the mound property was transferred to Pasco County in June 1989. Though the reconstruction and excavation lacked twenty-first-century technology that would have prevented invasive excavation and alteration, the Eschasakotes site remains one of the best-preserved examples of a temple mound. An ancient rock stele moved to another location, and the lithics provided additional clues

Two folks of Native American descent, Jamal and Queenie from DiamondLegacy, shared their experience of visiting the temple mound. Motivation for their visit was to locate an ancient rock stele carved by indigenous people who inhabited this territory. "As we both stood outside the fence stele, I asked a helpful gentleman nearby where the stele was removed from. He said the stele was originally positioned near the mouth of a major waterway, and a professional moving company delivered it there for the restaurateur. The restaurant [Johnny Leverock's Seafood House], where the stele was 'propped' had burned down and remained empty for more than a decade. He theorized that its misfortune may have been a curse resulting from the disturbance/relocation," related Jamal.

In 2002, Hedman reported on Johnny Leverock's Seafood House, where manager Joe Fulghum related how a boating channel was dredged and rocks were lifted out with a crane and piled on the adjacent land. The general

According to DiamondLegacy, "This particular rock stele is stated to have been carved by Aboriginal, Indigenous People....Reportedly, there are two faces carved on it....The stele was used for ceremonies." *Brother Jamal Richardson Bey and Queen Lillie, DiamondLegacyAmerica.org.*

theory was that the large rock was excavated during dredging of the channel. The restaurant chain started in 1948 and grew to twelve locations. The New Port Richey restaurant where the stele was situated had burned down in 2003, and the last of the chain was closed in 2006.

Whether it was the curse of the pharaohs from ancient Egypt or the practice of collecting Native American bones from burial locations, which resulted in the Graves Protection and Repatriation Act in 1990, the practice of retrieving bones of people evokes a gruesomely morbid aura, sometimes believed to be tied to misfortune. Thousands have been disturbed, and although the Oelsner Mound is the most well-preserved mound in Pasco County, virtually thousands of mounds marked the Gulf Coast of the peninsula, and a scarce few remain, meaning that everyone living on or near the west coast of Florida lives on or near an ancient Indian mound site. The mounds were demolished for their shell content, which was exhausted for road fill, while others were bulldozed for settlement and construction.

The other known sites identified in Pasco that hold aboriginal energy include the Hope Hammock Mound near Baillie's Bluff. It was named for Captain Samuel E. Hope. Legend has it that a surveyor named Peter Karr Baillie working in 1844 saved the son of a Seminole chief who, in turn, gifted him with the large ancient mound. Wells Sawyer excavated the mound, which measured twelve feet high, to the Weeden Island period. When the Beacon Square subdivision expanded north to Trouble Creek Road, the bulldozers hit the last vestige of Hope Hammock Mound as locals hunted the remnants for artifacts.

The Grace Memorial Gardens Mound was discovered in 1969 on the site of the cemetery of the same name on U.S. 19 in Hudson. Owner Melvin Sheer discovered it while excavation was taking place in the cemetery. Amateur archaeologists examined it, and they immediately found skeletons and tools. Sheer took artifacts, which were dated to 7500 BCE, to the University of Florida.

In east Pasco, the Lacoochee Mound near the present-day canoe rental area has been eradicated. Matthew Stirling from the Smithsonian dug into the mound in the 1930s, and by 1947, only a few badly decayed burials and potsherds remained.

Dayton remembers seeing the River Road Mound with the lithic scatter on land owned by Joe Collura as a teenager, although not much remains today of the River Road Mound.

In addition, Dayton actually identified the Evans Creek Mound from his own teenage expedition and filed a report with the Florida government. It was a substantial temple mound that was pulled down when Prospect Road was paved, Dayton explained. There is no trace of it today. It was indicative of the Lake Pasadena area, which Dayton described as a spot on the migration cycle, where the indigenous peoples would quarry fossilized coral for projectile points. Dayton remembered obtaining Jimmy Evans's permission to examine the mound, thus he named it for the property owner. When heavy rains came, Dayton saw an abundance of lithics.

9
New Port Richey

Fantasy and Silent Movie Legends

Thousands of years after settlement of the area known as Port Richey and New Port Richey by indigenous peoples, of which there is little recorded history, George R. Sims is considered the modern founder, as he became the owner of the Port Richey Company in 1916, having originally purchased the land with partner R.E. Filcher from P.L. Weeks. Four years earlier, Aripeka Sawmill sold part of its land to Weeks, his brother J.S. Weeks and W.E. Guilford. They formed the Port Richey Company with the goal of developing the lands. A Florida boomtown by the '20s, the city was incorporated in 1924. Regardless of the names, the Pithlachascotee River and the Gulf of Mexico were enticing, and the story of human experiences unfolded throughout time at these locations, and eventually institutions, came to fruition.

Two Extraordinary Men Have a Presence at the Richey Suncoast Theater

Without a doubt, the shadows of two twentieth-century men, Miracle Man and Mister Theatre, cast enormous silhouettes on the nearly one-hundred-year-old theater that has had several lives. These creative and hardworking men were Thomas Bell Meighan (1879–1936) and Willard Putnam Clark

Painting interpretation of the Thomas Meighan Theatre, which was named for the famous silent screen star of the Roaring Twenties in what was once coined the Hollywood of the East, New Port Richey. *Clinton Inman.*

(1906–1981). Because both of them were obsessively passionate about the theater, they might have known each other during their mortal lives, however their legacies and impact are felt in the theatrical world of New Port Richey. A portrait of Meighan, *The Miracle Man of Silent Film*, hangs in the theater lobby and watches over affairs, while a 1982 plaque dedicated to Clark is affixed to the front entrance, proclaiming, "Mister Theatre—A Patron of the Arts." (It was presented to his widow, Linda, to commemorate his work and dedication.) On any given visit to the Richey Suncoast Theatre, you may blink in disbelief as you spot the gorgeous haunted eyes of Meighan staring

A Haunted History of Pasco County

Thomas Meighan Theatre. *State Archives of Florida.*

at you or perhaps catch a glimpse of industrious Willard Clark hurriedly rushing by. If you dare to peruse seat BB1, you will feel a chill.

The Richey Suncoast Theatre began, not surprisingly, as the Thomas Meighan Theater. It was designed by Thomas Reed Martin for $75,000 and built by Richey Amusement Company under the auspices of George J. Becker and Warren E. Burns. At the opening on July 1, 1926, reporters said it was a Hollywood-type gala, and famous stars, such as Ed Wynn and Gloria Swanson, swept in. Thomas Meighan was called the "Miracle Man of Silent Screen," and his fame was monumental. He had just released a movie, *The New Klondike*, a story of Florida life in the liveliest of boom days, and many people thought Pasco County would become a colony for moviemaking and a haven for stars. Imagine the *Great Gatsby* as you think of the piano player accompanying Meighan's silent movie. Florida senator Jesse Mitchell acted as the master of ceremonies, and the crowd capacity was five hundred for the new theater, which was prematurely coined the Hollywood of the East. The momentous events of 1929 and the Great Depression would abruptly alter the anticipated course, and although Meighan remained a force until his death in 1936, he is remembered as an essential part of the era of the glamour of Hollywood. "In the spring of 1930, Thomas Meighan was present at the theater to push the button that would bring sound to the screen for local residents with the coming of the 'talkies.' New Port Richey was slated to become a new movie production center. However, it never reached fruition," wrote Adam J. Carozza in his thesis at University of South Florida in 2009.

William Maytum, former New Port Richey city councilman, said, "As I recall, it used to cost a dime admission. It was the only entertainment place we had in town." The theater building stood empty from 1964 to 1972. "The one-time movie theater stood vacant of theatrical activity since 1964, and is now active daily with paint brushes, ladders, laughter, arguments, dedication and gradual change of appearance," as reported in the *Tampa Tribune*'s article titled "Rebirth of a Theater—Young, Old Working Together" on May 12, 1972.

Mystery and folklore have encompassed the theater world since the time of Shakespeare. The Meighan Theatre has its share of mystifying aura that lingers with ghost hunters and paranormal investigators regularly visiting. An account of a man in the old projection room that housed the then 35 mm equipment was given in an article by Mark Beyer in 2005. It seems that when the worker returned with a baseball bat in hand to clobber the mysterious intruder, he had disappeared. An actor, Susan Nichols, noticed that objects had been rearranged, wrote Barbara L. Fredericksen in 2006. Jeff Cannon related that he had done shows at the theater: "I experienced the sound of glass breaking as I was preparing for a show there. I went looking for it, walked all around backstage, no one was there. I walked all the way up front to the box office and found one person working on tickets for that night's show."

The other ever-lingering ethereal presence at the theater is that of Mr. Clark, who routinely sat in seat BB1 to watch the performances. Not to diminish the extraordinary contribution of Clark to the New Port Richey area and to theater in Florida and perhaps the United States, there have in fact been reports of his ghostly presence since his passing. Clark has been spotted throughout the theater in the balcony, on the stage and in seat BB1. Susan Ostrom, who ran the Haunted Tours of New Port Richey, said, "Nobody seems to be afraid of him."

Charlie Skelton, who managed the theater, reported in a 2005 interview that actors had seen rumored apparitions in seat BBI, but the image was smiling and attentively watching the play. "I haven't seen the ghost though," Skelton said. "But he does seem to be a benevolent ghost. I guess he likes the theater in operation. Every once in a while, you come in and see a light on or maybe hear a noise." Folks who know the story sometimes ask to sit in seat BB1 for performances, and others pass by to take a look at it. One theory is that it was near an air conditioning vent, yet others report a presence in the area of seat BB1. Clark's contribution and dedication to the theater make the stories more than believable.

John Heagney reported in the *Pasco Times* on June 25, 1981, "Willard Clark, 74, died of an apparent heart attack…several hours after leaving his beloved Richey Suncoast Theater which he helped to organize. His pre-show chats with theater audiences were a fixture of each production." The memorial services were conducted at the theater as well. Clark was involved in local and regional theater for over fifty years and had served as the president of the theater board for three consecutive terms.

Marilyn Kalfus wrote a magnificent article about Clark's selfless contributions to New Port Richey in a 1980 tribute titled "Mr. Theater of Florida." She wrote, "There was magic in the air on August 25, 1972, opening night when the abandoned theater came alive…but there was nothing glamorous about some of the early problems that Clark faced. Clark recalled the seats were a pile of twisted debris and the roof leaked." A master electrician, Clark personally did all of the rewiring, and although he was not a youngster, he even climbed on the roof to patch it after the stage was flooded and the actors complained of getting wet. When one of the

Willard Clark, former president of the Richey Suncoast Theater (formerly Meighan Theatre) is said to hover at his favorite seat, BB1. *Author's collection.*

The ghost of Willard Clark is said to still roam the Richey Suncoast Theater. *Tampa Tribune.*

productions needed a stairway set, he ripped the spiral staircase out of his own riverfront house and delivered it to the set.

When Clark was slated to be honored at the twenty-fifth anniversary as a founder of the Florida Theater Conference in Daytona Beach, he lamented that the Richey theater would be in the middle of its production of *Funny Girl*, and he didn't know if he would make it. "The important thing to me is the show goes on," said Clark.

Clark's wife, Linda, didn't always accept her husband's compulsive devotion, and when their children, Willard Jr. and Ruth, were quite young, she asked him why he worked so many hours. Linda said Clark replied, "You will never know how important this theater will be to so many people—even lonely people. How it has brought people together."

Marc Swartsel, former president of the Arts Council, said, "Clark was the guiding light of the Richey Suncoast Theater." Perhaps when you visit, you will catch a flicker of that light.

Hacienda Hotel's Ambiance and Stories

The Hacienda Hotel at 5621 Main Street, New Port Richey, opened in the carefree, affluent decade of the Roaring Twenties, on February 4, 1927. In the midst of the Florida land boom, James Meighan, brother to silent film star legend Thomas Meighan, donated multiple building lots for the fifty-five-room masterpiece, and a mortgage loan was held for the elaborate furnishings of the Spanish-style hotel. With the economic downturn, stockholders were unable to meet payments and had to sell. The hotel changed hands several times, and in the late 1960s, two fires caused considerable damage.

By the 1980s, the Spiritual Church of Science and Revelations conducted regular healing and psychic services in the ballroom. Later in 1985, the Gulf Coast Jewish Family Services purchased the structure and backed $750,000 to renovate it as a geriatric treatment center. After it was nominated for the National Register of Historic Places in 1996, Lisa Jackson, Gulf Coast's planning manager, said, "What makes the property unique is its age and original sketches of design similar to the John Ringling's mansion." In a *Times* article on July 23, 1996, west Pasco historian Frances Mallett remembered when the Hacienda was "the place to be."

In 2006, a *Times* exposé reported that silent film star Gloria Swanson, famed defense attorney Clarence Darrow and baseball legend Babe Ruth were among hotel guests.

The hotel is an integral part of the community, so it was not surprising that the City of New Port Richey purchased it in 2004. Aware of the celebrated history and a swirl of slightly haunted tales about the Mediterranean

Hacienda Hotel first opened in 1927 as a haven for movie stars and other celebrities. *State Archives of Florida.*

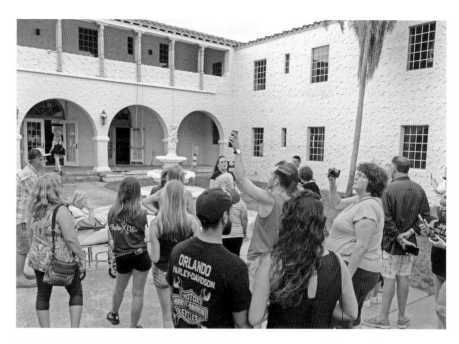

Above: Evie Parks and Derek Pontlitz of Poltlitz Asset Advisors, worked with West Pasco Historical Society to coordinate and deliver a self-guided historical ghost tour, which included the Hacienda Hotel. *Michele Miller, Courtesy of* Tampa Bay Times/*ZUMA*.

Left: Derek Furniss, project manager for construction in the renovation of the Hacienda, described coming in one morning just before Christmas to find discarded wood scraps assembled in the shape of a three-dimensional Christmas tree. *Nicole Berger-Ferro*.

structure, the city hosted a community Halloween party, as then city recreation director Elaine Smith found there was nothing for adults to do on Halloween. Later, in 2013, community cleanups were coordinated, with over 350 volunteers pulling weeds, yanking out carpet and scrubbing surfaces. The building was in limbo for a few years until Jim Gunderson, a Naples hotelier, received the top bid from the city for renovation in 2018. As of this writing, a reopening has yet to occur. "The hotel will be new when it opens," Gunerdon said, "but it will very much feel like you stepped back into the 1920s in an authentic way. It will feel like it's been here for ever and ever."

In 2009, during a stop on the Haunted History Tours of New Port Richey, operated by Susan Ostrom, people spotted a man in his fifties standing in the back window of the hotel and wearing a dress shirt. "At first," Ostrom said, "he appeared to be a security guard—but the building had been vacant for years. The man faced away as those who saw him got closer."

Nicole Berger-Ferro conducted ghost tours for the Friends of the Hacienda several times. With infrared cameras and sound devices, Berger-Ferro, who has been studying paranormal phenomena for thirteen years, found the Hacienda to be an upbeat space. In regard to ghostly rumors, there was no sign of a rumored legendary ghost figure named Matilda. Berger-Ferro's camera, however, showed the outline of a colorful dancing child who appeared to enjoy the heavy metal band Mötley Crüe's song "Home Sweet Home." Nicole, who said she always looks for logical explanations to justify mysterious events before coming to a conclusion, chuckled when she shared an observation that the carpenters wanted her to know. A discarded array of scrap wood pieces was strewn about at the end of the carpenters' workday while they were working on the second story, and the next morning, they noticed the pieces had been carefully assembled in a Christmas tree–like configuration. As it was nearing Christmas, they enjoyed the ghostly prank.

Legend of Chasco Might Have Shaken the Indigenous Peoples

Locals are not in a position to dispel illusion or eerie events, as townspeople, particularly leaders, have perpetuated falsified ethereal legend in the origin and evolution of the Chasco story for decades.

The Pithlachascotee River winds rhythmically through the heart of New Port Richey to the Gulf of Mexico. The setting is inspirational and a place that an artist would dream of painting or writing impressionistic interpretations about, not unlike the tales spun by the neighboring Weeki Wachee mermaids or stories of Tampa's fabled Gasparilla. As it was ripe for the picking at the height of the land boom, why not invent a fairytale origin story and raise some funds in the process? An immediate goal in 1922 was the need to build a permanent home for the Avery library.

Voila! A fabrication was born. Chasco was born in 1922, and although it originated as a small local event, it evolved into the major fundraiser for nonprofits and one of the largest attractions to lure people to New Port Richey.

The fable originated from Gerben DeVries, the first postmaster, who self-published *Chasco, Queen of the Calusas*. Supposedly, on New Year's Day 1922, while fishing on the banks of the river, DeVries discovered a clay pottery vessel, and like a message in a bottle, a story was concocted. Said to be in old Castilian Spanish and written by a priest named Padre Luis, the message told a tale of a Spanish boy and girl who were said to have been captured by the Calusa Indians in the vicinity, and after acceptance into the tribe, they were wed as Queen Chasco and King Pithla.

Although the Calusa tribe was in Florida, they were never in this area, and the Spanish and Calusa did not converge in New Port Richey. When the Spanish arrived, the indigenous people were the Tocobago, a confederacy of small Timucua splinter tribes. The Calusas lived along the southwest coast with Pineland Island in Charlotte Harbor as their center. Most of the Calusas died from disease soon after the Spanish arrived, so if a splinter band had been in the area, the story would have been of struggle and subsistence.

The Chasco Fiesta is now legend in its own right—a multiday annual event that is an enormous fundraiser that builds comradery and community enthusiasm. The director of the Chasco Fiesta pageant script for many years was Willard Clark.

The Chasco Inn

A part of the fabric of downtown and considered the oldest building on Main Street, the Chasco Inn replaced the Havens Building and was initially named the Rialto Hotel when constructed in 1915, with a name change to the Harmony Hotel in 1926. It housed a post office until 1927, as well as a restaurant, bus station and camera shop.

Modern-day look at Chasco Inn. *Author's collection.*

Mailia Bolster uses a FLIR thermal camera to detect paranormal activity in the old Chasco Inn. *Michele Miller, courtesy of* Tampa Bay Times/ZUMA Wire.

In September 1931, Mozelle Priest opened the former Justamere Inn with yet another name, the Chasco Inn, which seems to have stuck. According to the *Times*, it was "taking the name from the legend of New Port Richey." Bill and Margaret Weiskopf were owners in 1957, with a travel agency tucked into the second-floor hotel area.

Berger-Ferro picked up no paranormal activity at the inn, explaining that extensive renovation had replaced many original elements of the interior, making her task more challenging. Beth and Eric Fregger did extensive remodeling of the inn, which now houses eight businesses, including two restaurants. Berger-Ferro was informed that folks had seen the apparition of a priest walking the floors.

Reporter Michelle Miller wrote in July 2019 *Times* coverage that "purported sightings of a tall gentleman ghost clad in a black trench coat with a wide-brimmed hat [were] allegedly reported in one of the restaurants of the inn."

THE LAND OFFICE

In 1919, George R. Sims built the first brick building in New Port Richey at what is now 5728 Main Street. Originally intended for a bank, it contained a large masonry vault and decorative wood-framed windows and an extraordinary bookcase in the main office. It was sometimes referred to as the Milbauer Building for its longtime owners, realtor Michael L. Milbauer and lawyer Richard J. Milbauer. When Richard Milbauer died in 1981, he willed their estate of commercial property, valued at $3.1 million, to be divided equally between St. Leo University and the University of Florida.

The 1919 Sims building was first called the Land Office but also became known as the Milbauer Building, named for its longtime owners. *Author's collection.*

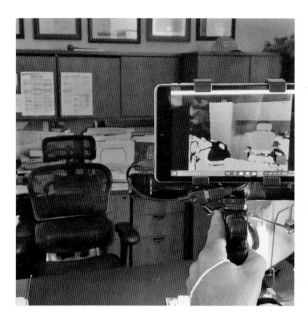

As Berger-Ferro employed infrared cameras in the office of Derek Pontlitz, she picked up a shadow of a friendly ghost on the office chair. *Nicole Berger-Ferro.*

To celebrate the centennial celebration of the gray brick building, Derek Pontlitz, who owns and operates an investment office at the site, coordinated a party and sponsored a historic walking tour complete with a guided ghost tour. Berger-Ferro spent time assessing the space and picked up on a happy apparition seated in outline form in the office area.

The meters went off in the safe room, which is now used as a coffee and break space, while a photo snapped of Evie Parks, the client relations specialist, shows the outline of a shadow who seems to be serving hors d'oeuvres. "Definitely some happy apparitions," said Berger-Ferro.

Meighan Mansion

Like ghosts of famous dramas *Phantom of the Opera, Beauty and the Beast* and *Cinderella*, the love of Thomas and Frances permeated their Meighan Estate on the banks of the Pithlachascotee and lingers in the communities there that share their name.

The Meighans were lured to New Port Richey by George R. Sims. Sims had purchased over ten thousand acres along the Pithlachascotee River. Meighan later invested in Sims's Hacienda Hotel, built on nine city lots that were donated by Thomas Meighan's brother, James.

A Haunted History of Pasco County

The Meighans built a house on the banks of the Pithlachascotee River and envisioned other stars coming to create a motion picture industry in New Port Richey. *State Archives of Florida.*

Pen-and-ink interpretation of the spectacular home that Thomas and Frances Meighan built on the banks of the Pithlachascotee River, frequented by stars such as Mary Pickford, Raymond Hitchcock, Gloria Swanson and Douglas Fairbanks. *Clinton Inman.*

Meighan's mansion on the banks of the river was in the Jasmine Point subdivision and included 640 feet of road frontage with an elegant formal entrance gate and pristinely landscaped groves. The thirteen bedrooms and six bathrooms with a gigantic swimming pool were designed for lavish entertaining. The home was demolished years ago, but the names of Thomas Meighan Estates and Meighan Courts remain, and many feel they are blessed by the overwhelming ghostly and ethereal spirit of love.

Karl Krug penned an extraordinary tribute to the love affair between Thomas and Frances just after Frances's death on January 16, 1951, in the *Pittsburgh Sun-Telegraph*. The title says it all: "Frances Ring's Death Writes an Ending to Meighan Love Idyll."

> *So, the Storybooks Tell: Frances Ring Meighan will be coming home in the Springtime to append the final chapter to one of the Theatre's prettiest and most enduring love stories.*
>
> *Everybody in show business, even in Hollywood where romance withers, dies and is reborn faster than the gossip columnists can keep up with it knew the devotion of Tommy Meighan and Frances Ring, the girl he met, courted and married when they were appearing in "The College Widow," back when the century was young. Everybody knew too, that they stayed married, and that she was at his side when the tall, handsome Pittsburgh Irishman died on the night of July 8, 1936 at their home in Great Neck.*
>
> *Tommy Meighan, the "miracle man" of the movies, whom William Powell once told me was the finest actor Pittsburgh ever produced and Frances Ring, the girl who became his wife, just as his fame was beckoning, lived an idyll—more fascinating than that conceived by the romanticists who penned their plays.*
>
> *Thus, if Death can ever write a "happy ending" and there are those who say that it can, the story of Tommy Meighan and Frances Ring will achieve that distinction when they bring her home in the Springtime and place her to rest beside the body of her famed husband in St. Mary's Cemetery in Lawrenceville.*
>
> *There isn't much room in the papers for even happy endings to real life stories in this era of atomic jitters and dime-a-dozen "romances" among the professional elite of the stuff, they're selling for entertainment.*
>
> *The accounts of the passing of Frances Ring Meighan might have said, for instance, that they spent their honeymoon in London where "The College Widow" repeated its tremendous American success*

Frances Ring and Thomas Meighan at their home in the height of the Roaring Twenties. *C. Heighton Monroe, public domain.*

and that Tommy returned in triumph to New York in a play called "Broadway Jones."

Then came the leading role in David Belasco's immortal, "The Return to Peter Grimm." Next the movies where following "The Miracle Man" in which he played a crook converted by a faith healer, his salary soared to $10,000 per week, and he became leading man for such stars as Mary Pickford, Normal Talmadge, Pauline Frederick and Marguerite Clark.

Throughout all these triumphs and more, the Meighans remained the sweethearts that dramatists dream of. She was his girl and he was her beau. Together they lived a serene, happy life while the shattered marriages of many friends and co-stars cavorted around on the front pages.

To end this nosegay and, perchance suggest an epitaph for the Meighans one need look only to Tom's own great triumph, "The Return of Peter Grimm." As a foreword to that fine fantasy, which he authored and produced, David Belasco wrote: "Love is the only thing that matters. It is the one thing that endures to the end."

Haunted Desk and William Barber with Civil War Letter

Christopher Martinez of the *Suncoast News* revealed the tale of a mid-nineteenth-century Winthrop desk. Volunteer Mary O'Benar at the West Pasco Historical Museum knew that the desk was donated by Bea Baum, a volunteer librarian. O'Benar periodically smelled smoke and even walked outside to see if someone was smoking near Orange Lake.

Informed about the olfactory hallucination, Baum admitted smelling cigar smoke and hearing noises—even the sense of a presence near the desk, proudly displayed at the museum. The desk originated from a 1903 courthouse in Hammond, Indiana, that had been razed in 1973 and then gifted to an Indiana historical society and exhibited at Lake County's fairgrounds for fifteen years. Reporter Mark Beyers found that it was next sold via auction to a new owner, allegedly Baum. As she prepared to move to Florida, Baum attempted to donate it to her local museum, but somehow, it wound up among her belongings in the moving truck. Discovering it among her transported belongings in Florida, she again donated it, this time to the museum in New Port Richey.

David Pace, president of the West Pasco Historical Society in 2009, allowed ghost hunters to visit the museum and check it out.

The desk of Civil War veteran William Barber was donated to West Pasco Historical Society in 1983 and dates to 1850. *West Pasco Historical Society.*

Tish Osborne reported in the *Tribune* in 2002 that volunteer Eve McMahan also discovered a letter in the desk written by William B. Barber of Company I, Ninety-Third Regiment, New York State Volunteers, dated June 20, 1862. O'Benar set out to find descendants of the soldier and asked permission of the historical board to return the letter to the family.

Erin Sullivan reported on a 2009 investigation in "A Ghost or Hoax?" about ghost hunters Erin Sullivan, Courtney Micalizzi, Sara Chapman and Nathan Thomas. With their recorder rolling, they posed some questions, hoping to capture electronic voice phenomena, known as EVPs. "They heard nothing and went home, thinking the night was a bust, but Thomas stayed up…going through the tape.…'I had no choice,' the hushed voice believed to be Union soldier Barber said, after Chapman asked how he felt about his desk being in the South.…At the end of the tape, Barber said, 'Where are you going? Come back.' Thomas couldn't believe it, they all had chills. 'I was shaking,' said Chapman, the founder of their paranormal investigating organization, Hunting the Haunted. She and Micalizzi have been ghost hunting for several years."

The White Heron Tea Room

Lewis Carroll wrote in *Alice in Wonderland*, "Yes, that's it! said the Hatter with a sign, it's always tea time." Tea, as in the peculiar children's fantasy, is intricately linked to mystery and fantasy. Whether it is Dame Agatha Chrisie or a tale from *Harry Potter*, tea is peripherally intertwined. The White Heron Tea Room on Grand Boulevard is not an exception to the norm.

Kelly Hackman, proprietor of the tearoom, says, "Downtown is a place of pride and community." With certifications as a tea specialist, she employs the etiquette and protocol of tea culture. The stunning shop in a vintage building is said to be frequented by the precocious spirit of a little girl who is rather active.

The White Heron Tea and Gift Shop is delightful, and occasionally, the energy of a resident is surmised. *Author's collection.*

When Berger-Ferro investigated the cozy little shop with her paranormal protocol and equipment, she admitted that she did feel some energy, but nothing specific.

Ordinance One

The city building now known as Ordinance One was built in 1939. Builders used some of the materials salvaged from the Ralph Werner building of 1921, which housed Bill Casey's Barber Shop, the Central Market and Beach's Music Store. The building was occupied by the city hall, town library and the volunteer fire department.

Stylishly restored by Bob Carroll, it houses a trendy pub and has been renovated to reveal open rafters and exposed brick. Berger-Ferro enjoyed her experience in Ordinance One during the ghost tour. Berger-Ferro explained that two entities were eager to talk to her through her EVP and made contact rather quickly. When she asked if she could talk to them, one quipped, "What now?" The general demeanor of the interaction led her to conclude they might be firefighters and were chums.

Ordinance One in downtown New Port Richey served as former city hall and later firehouse. *Author's collection.*

10

Zephyrhills

The Retired Civil War Colony and Its Legends

Zephyrhills celebrated its centennial in 2010. By way of development, Simon J. Temple, who had many business dealings throughout Florida, purchased acreage in 1886 from the Florida Railway and Navigation Corporation. He named the original town after Dr. Joseph M. Abbott. It was abundant with virgin pine and was believed to be a wonderful agrarian area.

Captain Howard B. Jeffries and his son-in-law, Raymond Moore, purchased 3,500 acres of the land in 1909, and the Zephyrhills Colony Company was formed. Divided into 5-acre tracts and placed on the market, one section was laid out into town lots. With simple newspaper advertising, thousands of acres were sold. The great majority of the settlers were Union soldiers. (Jeffries had enlisted as a private in the Twenty-Eighth Pennsylvania Infantry, Company F, and later served as captain of the Seventy-Second Black Infantry, which was organized in Covington, Kentucky, before he mustered out.)

The area grew with an agrarian base and eventually garnered a reputation as a haven for "tin can tourists," as seasonal visitors camped in the town and enjoyed its amenities. Stories abound of the frontier from open range to small-town life.

A Friendly Ghost Roams the 1911 Howard B. Jeffries House on Fifth Avenue

Chuckling, Eileen Anne "Annie" Westermann remembered that children in the neighborhood readily referred to it as "the haunted house" when she and Steven Herman purchased the quaint, yet dilapidated, house in 1992. The renovation and care of the house was a labor of love but did give the couple an occasional surprise. Jeffrey Brainard reported in a 1995 *Times* article, "When they've been alone in the house, Steve and Annie have heard doors slamming and felt breezes—and there's no one there. Pictures have flown off the wall. And one morning a cleaning woman said she saw a strange man, dressed in black who was smiling."

Westermann said they liked old houses, and this one embodied Zephyrhills history. "'I feel it's something you give the community' she said of the project…'And I would like to think the ghost of Captain Jeffries is smiling because he likes the result.'"

In 1997, attorney Steven Herman said he was working late upstairs and heard something large fall downstairs and, on investigation, found nothing. "The occurrences aren't really sightings," said Christina Barnes, secretary and previous chairman of Founders Day, "but rather feelings that someone is present. I have heard things but then there was nothing there but a feeling of a presence."

Captain Howard B. Jeffries, a Civil War veteran, sits with his wife, Helen Mar Jeffries, on the porch of his home. His vision was a colony as a haven for veterans of the Grand Army of the Republic (GAR). *Zephyrhills Depot Museum.*

Jeffries still roams the two-story house he built in 1911 in Zephyrhills, or is it Helen who died in the house in 1931? *Ernest E. Wise.*

Westermann said the process of completing the documentation of the house for placement in the National Register of Historic Places was involved and tedious, but it was so deserving for the extraordinary house made of heart of pine that must have been the most spectacular of houses in early pioneer Florida.

More recently, since the city purchased the historic home, Gail Hamilton, community redevelopment director, has felt the ghostly presence. She heard a voice utter, "What are you doing?" and felt warm breath on her neck.

If indeed there is a ghost, is it Captain Jeffries or perhaps his dear wife, Helen Mar Jeffries, who died in the house on February 23, 1931? She was beloved by the town, and merchants closed their shops for her funeral. Or perhaps Howard is still haunted by the memories of the Civil War and consoles himself in the ghostly comfort of his beloved home. Westermann further speculated that it might even be the adoring presence of the subsequent owner, Helen Hamilton Hart, a retired schoolteacher and beloved community member who took such painstaking care of the yard and grounds with native plants that she worked hard to maintain.

Georg Karl Tanzler and the Macabre Sleeping Beauty in Zephyrhills

The most sinister of dark local fairytales is that of Georg Karl Tanzler, who was born on February 8, 1877, in Dresden, Germany, and died in Zephyrhills on July 3, 1952. Like Baron von Frankenstein, he was challenged to create a human-like figure. Did he possess narcissism, delusion, profound obsession or necrophilia, or was his case truly a love story?

Tanzler was consumed with a dream in his native Germany that compelled him to search the world over for the "beautiful lady of his vision," he told the *Key West Citizen* in 1940.

Fifty-four-year-old Tanzler claimed he was estranged from his wife and family. He married thirty-year-old Anna Doris Schäfer (his one and only marriage) on November 20, 1919, in Dresden. While serving as a medic in World War I, he garnered acclaim for his ability to assist surgeons with reconstruction of soldiers' faces that had been shattered in combat, although he was not a doctor. He immigrated through Ellis Island in 1922, leaving a toddler daughter and his pregnant wife in Germany, although his wife followed in 1926 and settled in Zephyrhills, while Tanzler served as an X-ray technician in Key West, working at the Marine Hospital.

From an appointment at Marine Hospital, Elena Hoyos Mesa was sent to the X-ray technician at the hospital, namely Tanzler. "She was gorgeous—dark-eyed, nineteen-year-old, slender Cuban brunette," said Mike Capuzzo in the *Miami Herald* of 1931. Astonished at the sight of Elena, who mirrored his long-sought-after dream image, he proceeded with the evaluation. The rudimentary film was indisputable—end-stage, acute tuberculosis. He set out to cure Elena with radiation. Considered miraculous, radium was routinely placed in toothpaste, makeup, chocolate bars, medicines and water at the time. (Wilhelm Röntgen discovered radiation in 1895 as he observed that X-rays penetrated through to react with barium.) Marie Curie named it radioactivity and used a mobile X-ray machine in the battlefields of World War I. As they were unaware of the dangers at the time, precautions were not taken.

Curie's papers and even her cookbook remain too highly radioactive to handle. Victims, like the Radium Girls, who painted clock dials with radium, succumbed to painful deaths.

In a nearly stalking fashion, Tanzler ingratiated himself with Elena and her family and treated her with radiation and a concoction of gold

Left: Karl Tanzler believed radiation would be a miracle cure. *Photo by Stetson Kennedy in 1940, Florida Keys Public Library.*

Right: The object of an infamous obsession, lovely seventeen-year-old Elena Hoyos Mesa poses in 1926. *Photo by Stetson Kennedy, Florida Keys Public Library.*

water. He lavished gifts on her and her impoverished family, but when he proposed marriage, Elena's father realized something was awry and banished him.

Elena succumbed to death with a seizure at a Halloween parade in 1931. When he heard the news, Tanzler rushed to her house and attempted to revive her for hours. He believed he had found his life's dream, only to lose her.

Eight years later, Tanzler received international publicity when the body of Elena was found in his tumbledown shack. Public opinion viewed him as a Don Quixote figure. A book, *A Halloween Story*, was published by Rod Bethel and contained his rambling diary. Ben Harrison penned the book *Undying Love* and then wrote a song of the same title that received acclaim.

After Elena's death, Tanzler had maneuvered his way to fund a mausoleum for her, of which only he had the key, and then he abducted her body. Meticulously reconstructing her decaying body and experimenting further with radiation in failed attempts to revive her, he serenaded her every evening with melodious organ music (on a pipe organ he built

This air machine device was constructed by Tanzler to catapult his love into eternity. *Edith McGavern.*

himself) and dressed her in bridal finery, jewels and daily fresh flowers. When police, with the help of Elena's sister, Florinda Medina, found the corpse in 1940, it was a doll-like configuration of papier mâché, wax, cheesecloth, piano wire, chemicals and glass eyes. In the yard was a portion of a strange, dilapidated airplane fuselage that was labeled in his photo album as "Elena's air ship to Heaven."

Tanzler reveled in the publicity and responded to the bizarre recognition. He exaggerated his background, claiming he was a count born in a haunted castle with nine college degrees and demanding to be addressed as doctor and to attach "von Cosel" to his name. The dean of Key West's lawyers volunteered to defend him, and he quickly discovered that the statute of limitations had run out on grave robbery charges. When the astute judge questioned Tanzler's sanity, even his estranged wife in Zephyrhills, Doris, wrote a letter to the authorities in Key West attesting to his peculiar behavior but affirming his sanity. As Tanzler's case was heard, he asked the magistrate, Judge W.V. Albury, to "return the body to him." The judge was aghast as Tanzler had no legal claim on the body, and although he was forced to dismiss the charges of grave robbery because the statute had expired, he rebuked Tanzler and returned Mesa's body to her sister, who arranged for a secret burial in a location that has never been disclosed.

Despite media, coroner and police reports, as well as evidence, folks were enamored with the one-sided love story. Money poured in for a fund to entomb the corpse in a glass case, and when Tanzler claimed that he would do a nationwide tour with the corpse, he was contacted by a movie agent. The Lopez Funeral Home put Elena on display, and within three days, 6,850 people came from all over the country to pass the bier and view the girl doll in the blue rayon robe. Unfortunately, it would be many years before the torrid and depraved story of stalking came to the light of day.

"You couldn't sleep for weeks once you'd seen the body," the attorney for Elena's family said. "It hounded me for years and years," Capuzzo reported.

Not deterred, Tanzler, who had been fired from his job at Marine Hospital, gave tours of his ramshackle house for ten cents and later lived on welfare until he moved his laboratory to Zephyrhills (where his sister, wife and surviving daughter lived) in 1941. He lived there for the rest of his life.

A local Zephyrhills community member and avid keeper of local history gave the author an insight into Tanzler's life in Zephyrhills. Edith "Edi" Nell Austin McGavern said: "I have personal and family information on the Karl Tanzler story. My father, Arthur Austin, local high school class of 1930, regularly recounted his experience with Tanzler. [Austin, in his adult life, served as a missionary/minister and cofounder of the Fundamental Church in Zephyrhills.] Rumors abounded of Tanzler, and my father, as boys will do…he and his teenage buddies ventured out to take a look at the Tanzler place one evening. Tanzler lived on Twenty-Third Street just north of Highway 54. There, at his place, was a giant airplane that he had towed to Zephyrhills [with eight-foot tires] when he arrived along with the sound of loud Gothic-style pipe organ music that emanated every evening from his home."

Tanzler made a meager income repairing church pipe organs and lived in his sister's house. Ella Tanzler Duzan came through Ellis Island from Dresden in 1920 and died in 1943 in Zephyrhills.

Edi continued, "On this particular evening, the curiosity-seeking boys, with my father in tow, peered into the window of Tanzler's tiny three-room house with the sign affixed to the door that read, 'DR. CARL VON COSEL'S LABORATORY.' Keenly protective of his place, Tanzler spotted the boys right off, and much to their surprise, invited the fellows to come in for a visit. A few cordialities, and he divulged that he was in the very midst of conducting a séance. Tanzler further conveyed, 'There was a man with red hair named George who was killed in World War I, present in spiritual form who wished to speak with one of the boys.'"

Edi said that Arthur's mouth flew open as hair-raising panic ensued. You see, Arthur's deceased uncle George fit those parameters. Edi related that her father bolted for the door and ran for his life until he reached his home in Zephyrhills. "It was one of those stories that Dad recounted many times," she said.

Coincidentally, this practice of curiosity-seekers visiting Tanzler's compound continued until Tanzler's death in 1952, to which Edi's husband, Cecil McGavern, could attest. It is interesting that both Edi's father, Arthur Austin, and her husband's father, Cecil G. McGavern (Zephyrhills High School class of 1930), were ministers in Zephyrhills.

Edi recalled that there was another side of the Tanzler story that was not publicized—a painful story of his family and their survival. She talked so fondly of his dear wife, Doris. "Generations of our family were friends with his wife, daughters and granddaughter," she said. She explained that Tanzler and Doris had two daughters—one, named Crystal, who died of diphtheria at age five. Edi added, "Crystal was buried in Oakside Cemetery in Zephyrhills. The grave marker had a beautiful angel on it, which was later stolen."

Born in Dresden on September 7, 1889, Doris was described as spunky, with white, curly hair. Edi recalled, "She spoke with a very heavy German accent." Edi's grandmother, Emma Kruse Plank (wife of Finis Plank), was a neighbor and friend to Doris and "they lived just two miles from each other on Forbes Road in Zephyrhills." Edi added that at that time it was not known as Forbes Road, as it was given that name after the next owners who bought Emma Plank's home. "Doris and Emma were both born in Germany and shared a common bond of German heritage. They loved to converse in their native tongue of German; in fact, folks said they were the only two German speakers in Zephyrhills. Doris even presented my grandmother with some precious china of German origin." Doris died in 1977 at the age of eighty-seven. An upstanding citizen, she was a member of the First United Methodist Church and had lived in Zephyrhills for fifty years at the time of her death. She and her surviving daughter, Ayesha, withstood a horrendous shadow cast on them by Tanzler. History would attest to the benevolence of the Zephyrhills community and folks like Emma Plank who were there for them as neighbors.

Doris's surviving daughter, Ayesha Paulina Tanzler, was Edi's mother's age and a close friend. Ayesha later married, and her only daughter was the same age as Edi's sister, so this third generation continued the bonds of friendship. For a short time, Doris's granddaughter also lived with Edi's grandmother. (Edi's grandmother had been a schoolteacher at the one-room school in Wesley Chapel and was well equipped to step in when the family needed her.) "While the granddaughter resided with Emma, Tanzler would walk the several miles to my grandmother's house and visit with his only granddaughter. He was not allowed to come into the house with his sordid past, but he often sat on the porch and visited with his granddaughter under the tutelage of Emma," Edi said.

Edi recalled that Tanzler's appearance was consistent with newspaper accounts. He had a long white beard and always wore a heavy black wool suit and tennis shoes without socks.

The *Dade City Banner* reported on August 15, 1952, "Tanzler who once kept the body of a dead woman in his home for five years, until its discovery in 1940, was found dead in his home in Zephyrhills on Wednesday morning."

Pasco County deputy sheriff Gene Rossi, who was summoned to the scene by an anxious neighbor, determined that Tanzler had been dead for about three weeks prior to the discovery of his body. The paper continued, "Tanzler, 75, lived alone in a three-room house about two miles north east of Zephyrhills. He was last seen alive on July 22. A neighbor, George A. Pattison, living about two hundred feet east of Tanzler's house, notified the sheriff's office Wednesday that Tanzler's mail was accumulating and that the door to his house was locked."

Doris was called to settle the estate of her estranged husband in late 1952. Peering inside his place exposed a life-sized plaster-of-Paris effigy of a young woman. He had once again sought comfort from his doll-like image of the woman he stalked and revered. Edi explained that Tanzler was known to have made many death masks of Elena, so it wasn't too far-fetched to believe that he would re-create her in wax or papier mâché form.

Perhaps this most notorious of haunted Zephyrhills stories was the work of a haunted man, or in retrospect, one wonders if the constant experimentation of high-dose radiation affected the rationality of Tanzler. Without a doubt, the legend of Tanzler lives on in Zephyrhills.

Arthur Boardman Storms's Tombstone States, "He Died as He Had Lived in the Defense of the Right"

Storms met an untimely death at age fifty-one. A hardworking baker and owner of the Home Bakery, which he built in 1912, he was the first on the scene at the American State Bank just after an explosion caused by

Storms's life was cut short as he heroically took on six bank robbers. His tombstone reflects his bravery. *Ernest E. Wise.*

six notorious bandits who cut the telegraph lines and traumatized the town. He slipped into the alley behind the bank, and firing his rifle, he hit one of the six bandits. Storms was then gunned down with a shotgun at close proximity and died instantly. Leaving his wife, Lahala Sue, and five children, his life was cut short with unfinished business in the new Zephyrhills colony.

Explosives cracked the building, and even today, while walking down Fifth Avenue at the Daniels block, folks occasionally claim they smell an aroma of sourdough bread or look up from their cellphones at the sound of a popping with no explanation.

Professor Morris Museum

Professor Austin B. Morris, an accomplished horse trainer/veterinarian from New York, and his wife, Melissa Jane, opened the Professor Morris Museum in 1913 at the corner of Fifth Avenue and Second Street (the house no longer exists but is near the present site of the Alice Hall Community Center on Highway 54). His collection of taxidermy and artifacts made of animal bone was a curiosity that provided an education but also occasionally nightmarish contemplation.

The Morris Museum was a curiosity of all types of taxidermy that was started by a retired horse veterinarian and his wife. *Zephyrhills Depot Museum.*

His obituary said, "In early life he manifested great love for all animals on his father's farm." A famous horse veterinarian, A.B. Morris worked in Canada in 1875 and treated over fifteen thousand horses. Later, in Paulding, Ohio, he was paid a whopping $10,000 (a fortune in the day) for saving an irreplaceable stallion. He moved to Zephyrhills and opened the museum, which was jam-packed with profound taxidermy and included furniture, chairs and even a wagon made from the bones of all kinds of animals. It seems that over the years, he had saved the bones from many of the animals he treated that met their demise. In 1914, he received acclaim in Zephyrhills for mounting a twelve-foot, five-hundred-pound alligator.

"This town can boast of having one of the best miniature museums in existence. Professor Morris, a veterinary surgeon, the owner, and he only charges ten cents to go through it. It will surely make a person sit up in amazement to see the variety of articles contained in it," read a 1914 *Tribune* article.

A horseshoe was always affixed to the door because it was believed that witches feared horses and would be turned away by a door with a horseshoe mounted on it with the points up for good luck.

Grand Army of the Republic and Woman's Club

The Grand Army of the Republic Hall on Eighteenth Street, just north of Sixth Avenue, and the Woman's Club, which sits to the east of the Captain Jeffries home, are also plagued by an occasional eerie presence. Union veterans and townspeople constructed the largest frame building in the county in 1910 as a meeting place for Garfield Post 39. Today, Zephyr Post 118, American Legion Hall, occupies the space, which also served as a church, city hall, concert hall and movie theater throughout the years. The Grand Army of the Republic was one of the largest special interest groups in the United States after the Civil War, and Zephyrhills often hosted the annual encampments. The building has hardwood floors and an array of settling noises that can frighten the unsuspecting visitor.

The Woman's Club was built in 1932 by the Works Progress Administration (WPA) from native rock hauled from a quarry on the Hillsborough River, as were the other area Depression-era buildings, although the actual club dates to 1915. During the worst days of the Great Depression, deprivation was everywhere. The Woman's Club building is a legacy to the survival instinct of the country, and one cannot drive up Fifth Avenue without glancing at that magnificent limestone structure that holds so many secret stories.

A former president of the club, Juanita Goeden, shared the story of an evening when she was setting up decorations for the fashion show to occur the next day. Alone in the building, she said it was just creepy. "I couldn't wait to finish my projects and leave, as there were noises, gusts of air, and at the very least, the feeling of a place that has housed the gamut of memories—joys and sadness."

In 2003, a major renovation was in the works. Bruce Mills of Old Thyme Carpentry & More said the fireplace, which had been closed for years, would be restored and opened.

11
WESLEY CHAPEL

THE FEUD AND MORE

Wesley Chapel, previously known as Gatorville and Godwin, is a burgeoning area that is sometimes called New Tampa, as the blurring county lines between Hillsborough and Pasco are settled by suburbanites.

Settlement began in the 1840s, with a handful of homesteaders coming to take advantage of land from the Armed Occupation Act of 1842. A small influx of settlers arrived after the Civil War, but lumber trusts from the likes of John D. Rockefeller, Otto Hermann Kahn and Edwin Wiley Grove held the land and depleted the timber in the 1900s.

Largely agrarian, moonshining, open range, timber/turpentine and gator-hunting stories fill the pages of a sparsely populated history. Double Branch Baptist Church was the host for Fifth Sunday Sings and singing convention, which was a cultural event in the South in the late nineteenth century.

THE NOTORIOUS FEUD OF ELLIS AND GILLETT FAMILIES

A traffic light on State Road 54, west of I-75, marks a curve known among old-timers as the haunted Tom Ellis Curve, and a tombstone at the County Line Cemetery memorializes it. The feud came to a head on July 4, 1909. Preston Gillett borrowed his mother's buggy and old white mare and was driving near Quail Hollow Boulevard. He happened on Tom Ellis and, as was custom in the day, reluctantly offered him a lift in the wagon. With

The tombstone inscription on the marker of Thomas M. Ellis (often called the curse of the tomb) at the County Line Cemetery perpetuates the feud of Ellis and Gillett. *Ernest E. Wise.*

their sordid history, few words were exchanged as they approached what is now known as Ellis Curve (where Walgreens stands on Highway 54). Ellis motioned for Gillett to halt and let him off. Suspicious of Gillett, Ellis had his hand on his shotgun. Sure enough, in a few short paces, Ellis spun around with his pistol drawn to gun down Gillett, but Gillett rose up the shotgun and blasted Ellis into oblivion.

The tomb of Ellis was inscribed by his father, "Let them perish that were against me and be covered with shame and dishonor." All versions of the story say that Ellis had a reputation as a bandit in the county. Gillett readily confessed to shooting Ellis, but Sheriff Bart turned a blind eye to the crime and presented Gillett with two shotgun shells to reimburse him.

John M. Taylor has written a short story, "A True Crime from Pasco County," in which he details the events of the feud that lasted for many years. He stated, "In 1907 killings in the deep woods over women or moonshine were all too common and Tom Ellis was known to favor both."

To summarize the story related to the author by ninety-one-year-old rancher/historian Bill Smith of Wesley Chapel in 2017, Tom Ellis's brother, Deputy Lee Ellis, was married to the beautiful Melinda "Lindy" Ellis. Lee had warned his brother to refrain from the inappropriate behavior and obvious obsession he had with his wife, gorgeous Lindy. Tom first murdered Lindy's brother Auston Gillett because he had supposedly been a witness when Tom had previously murdered Ben Stafford. Lindy and her children adored Uncle Auston, but charges were never brought.

Just days later, Tom murdered his own brother, Lee, at the front counter of the company store. It was a stray bullet, circumstantial evidence, so once again, no charges were filed. Frantic with fear, Lindy fled to New Orleans with her best friend, Sally.

The animosity accelerated between both families. "Shoot on sight," was declared by Sheriff Bart, frustrated that one of his deputies had been gunned down and not brought to justice. "Family ties are stronger than reason, and Tom's death left behind a bitter quarrel between the Ellis and Gillett families. Until the end, Richard Ellis believed his son Tom was the victim," said Taylor.

Many believe both the Tom Ellis Curve and the County Line Cemetery are haunted with the tortured spirit of the murderer and his victims.

Hidden Young Pilots Lost in the Swampy Woods for Decades

Twelve enthusiastic young soldiers with their lives ahead of them met their fate in the rugged frontier terrain of central Pasco. They included ten men of the 488th Bomber group from MacDill Field flying a B-17 Flying Fortress on February 28, 1944. Two men flying P-51 Mustangs from Bartow Army Airfield experienced a midair collision on June 8, 1945.

Entry into World War II came abruptly, and Florida was vulnerable with German U-boats in the Gulf of Mexico. There was a push to become proficient in munitions industries, which had lagged since the Great War. In Florida, 172 army air bases were built, including Zephyrhills and Hillsborough Army Air Bases. They were populated with youth in training, and the spirit of patriotism was high.

Hidden in the Florida wilderness since those tumultuous war years, amid the cypress, pines and palmettos, are crash sites, some of which are yet to be discovered.

A Boeing B-17 took off at 9:00 p.m. on the evening of February 28, 1944, and after two hours of flying, the control tower radioed for the plane

Above: Historic hangar at MacDill, where the fated plane occupied space for upkeep and maintenance. *Ernest E. Wise.*

Left: Lost in the deep woods were nine young soldiers. Courier Journal.

to return. Through a series of events, during which it was believed that the plane was approaching MacDill Air Force Base, it struck a path of trees and crashed on K-Bar Ranch, killing nine fliers. The B-17 careened into the terrain, broke up and burst into flames. The debris was scattered over the semi-wooded area in a distance of 520 yards. Fire broke out immediately, and only Gunnery Sergeant Norman was able to escape. Killed in this crash close to the midnight hour of the leap year were Bill Alsabrock, Donald G. Barber, Larice Boyle, Twyman Harper, John Ligon, Arthur O'Connor, Ernest Palm, Lawrence Siers and Roy Stroh. The accident site was discovered the following day at noon, and on March 1, rancher Isaac Andrew "I.A." Krusen signed off on the report. The story was then filed in archives until the twenty-first century, when accident reports and photos were reexamined by one of the descendants.

In addition, two P-51 Mustangs made contact in a midair collision at about nine thousand feet on June 8, 1945. One plane impacted near I-75 and I-52, while the other plummeted south of Bellamy Road, and the pilots who had been friends, John Terry and Robert Walker, perished.

With the passage of time, the deep woods of the area are being uncovered with settlements, and the stories are being divulged by Linda Rodgers, the niece of co-captain John Ligon. Perhaps over time, the resting places of other brave soldiers will be revealed from their hiding places in the underbrush.

Lewis Van Dercar and His Place Called Enchantment in Wesley Chapel

Dressed in a majestic black cloak and horned crown, Lewis Van Dercar welcomed up to three thousand people from across the country to attend the annual Halloween festivities at his Wesley Chapel "hideaway" named Enchantment, which was a living museum to his talented artwork. His self-proclaimed status was warlock and prince of the Order of Magi, and he had mysterious powers, specifically extrasensory perception and the power to levitate.

Van Dercar explained that he was a blend of the *Wizard of Oz*, hobbits from *Lord of the Rings*, *Alice in Wonderland* and *Camelot* and that he wanted to personify the supernatural in a kind of magic place at his home.

As he was always the spinner of odd tales with an enormous sense of humor, folks remembered the advertisement he posted in 1961 to sell his poltergeist. He explained that he had purchased a new table for his study, which had been used in a stage play of *Arsenic and Old Lace*, and discovered it was possessed by a female poltergeist. He tolerated Polter until she started leaving marks on his paintings. "If she could paint, I would not object," he said, "but the fact is she's really terrible." The advertisement explained that the table wouldn't go with her, as he would employ ancient ritualistic rites, and he had been reading up on the method to transfer her.

In 1973, he wanted to leave heavily populated Miami. The *Palm Beach Post* wrote, "Lewis van Dercar, creator, sculpture, prankster, and free-thinker—is leaving his landmark home in downtown Miami after fifty years and moving

Van Dercar named his house and grounds the enchanted forest, as it was full of his sculptures. *Ernest E. Wise.*

to a farm where he won't feel so 'cornered up'…leaving a vacuum that probably won't be filled.…Magic city is losing some of its soul."

When his friends told him that he might not do so well in a rural, redneck area with his exotic ideas, he said he would be fine. Reflecting back on the move to Glidewell, he explained that he knew he would be okay after his first encounter with a Pasco County sheriff's deputy: "We spent three hours discussing philospher Schopenhauer, and I decided I would do all right."

Van Dercar also hosted legendary Friday night open houses at his place at 2590 Queen Sago Place, which he built by himself. It was adorned with whimsical, original sculptures of various sizes and themes, including gargoyles and gnomes. Friends, metaphysicians, witches and the curious entered the wrought-iron gates framed with massive eight-foot gargoyles. He constructed a geodesic dome house, covered in ivy, which also emcompassed the two hundred statues. An exterior wall of the house features faces of every age and culture—Greek gods; sea monsters; heroines; gargoyles; Moses; and faces from Egypt, India, China and many other places.

Van Dercar was born in Detroit and entered the U.S. Navy during the Great Depression to help his family and served in the merchant marine in World War II, working for a time as an aircraft engineer. After his time in the

A gargoyle sculpture by the warlock Van Dercar stands guard at his home. *Ernest E. Wise.*

Touched by the losses at the 1972 Munich Olympics, Van Dercar paid tribute to the athletes in the sculpture of the hand. *Ernest E. Wise.*

Left: Lewis Van Dercar's place in Wesley Chapel hosted massive annual Halloween events on the grounds. Van Dercar claimed to have mysterious powers. *Ernest E. Wise.*

Below: Van Dercar moved to Pasco from Miami to create a studio. *Ernest E. Wise.*

service, he moved to Miami, where his entry into art was through hands-on jobs, as he was an animator for the *Popeye* cartoon.

In an interview with his grandson, Bobbie Ebie Van Dercar, in 2015, Bobbie explained that his grandfather was frequently compared to Andy Warhol and painted and sculpted in a variety of art mediums, including oils, multidimensional paintings and his own technique of sculpture, which were used in numerous public locations, such as parks and zoos, and were still valued and collected posthumously. Bobbie still proudly displayed an innovative sculpture that his grandfather was inspired to do in honor of the athletes lost in the 1972 Munich Summer Olympics.

Van Dercar died quietly in his sleep on December 15, 1988, with his wife of fifty years, Lady Margaret Houston Van Dercar, by his side. Like a modern-day Merlin, sculptor Lewis Van Dercar created an enchanted forest where Halloweens and supernatural celebrations were abundant.

The Road to Nowhere

The Road to Nowhere, dissecting Wesley Chapel, was lonely and secluded, and for most of its history, it was a daunting road to navigate. For over twenty-five years, it remained an unfinished dead end, and even after it was completed from Wesley Chapel to Tampa, it continued to be referred to, similarly by the State Road Department, as the Road to Nowhere, although maps marked it State Road 581 or Thirtieth Street Extension from Tampa. Built in 1959, it was part of the deal to acquire land for the new University of South Florida, although it started at the campus and wandered through miles of wild and undeveloped countryside, including three ranches, coming to an abrupt dead end at the county line in a cow pasture.

It was an embarrassment for Hillsborough officials. In 1971, the U.S. Department of Transportation decided to construct an overpass at the county line for Interstate 75, under the contingency that both counties would complete their portions of the road. For Pasco County in 1971, it was the next-to-last priority for road construction. By 1977, it was still not completed.

Journalist Dale Wilson included the Road to Nowhere in his piece about comedian Red Buttons, suggesting that it be used in his customary monologue on strange things. "There's the overpass that nobody claims lying at the end of the Road to Nowhere that may end up as the Bridge that Never Was."

Known as Bruce B. Downs (now running from State Road 54 in south-central Pasco County) since its renaming in 2000, the road had other chilling notoriety. Glidewell wrote that it was dubbed the Road to Nowhere so long ago that no one really remembered whether the name was an accusation of political boondoggling or a comment on the fact that so many people had ridden along it to oblivion, in reference to the numerous murdered bodies discovered on its roadsides.

In the mid- to late 1970s and 1980s, there were at least a dozen murders, most of them women, in which the victims were either killed or dumped along State Road 581 or along other rural roads branching off from it. Several bodies were found by hunters in the wooded sections off the road. Two bodies were victims of serial killer Gerald Stano. Charles Carskaddon of Missouri is believed to be one of the eight victims of a pair of female serial killers, part of the highway killings. In 1989, this was commonplace.

Today, it is a four-lane highway with bustling traffic, and only the veterans remember the clandestine history of the Road to Nowhere.

12
Lacoochee Lore

A company town, Lacoochee was left empty-handed with the closing of Cummer Cypress Company in 1959. Its roots go back to 1888, when two railroads were completed, and abundant citrus groves and strawberry crops produced a thriving town on the Withlacoochee River, until hard freezes in 1895. It got a second wind when Jacob Cummer from Michigan opened the sawmill in 1922. As the majestic trees were felled, the sawmill closed and the town transformed, yet the devout, prideful remembrances embrace its history.

Lillian Hartley Met Her Demise July 1, 1924, in Lacoochee as Her Husband Rammed a Racing Locomotive

The group left early from a fishing trip at the Withlacoochee River to avoid a heavy cloud that was threatening rain. Lillian's husband, William, stopped just before the railroad crossing to drop off one of the guests, and as he turned toward the track, he glimpsed a car parked parallel to the tracks. Distracted by the car, he didn't acknowledge the rushing locomotive from the Seaboard Air Line Train hammering down the track. William moved up the steep grade to the track. By the time he heard the engine sounds, it was too late. He was aghast to see the train on them.

The train traverses through Lacoochee. *State Archives of Florida.*

The engineer was helpless to avoid striking the car, which whirled in a circle and catapulted over the side of the abutment with a vicious wallop. The horror-stricken train crew and neighbors leaped to help the injured. With a broken ankle, serious lacerations and a fractured skull, Lillian fought to survive but succumbed to death three days later. At age forty-five, Lillian was a socialite and consummate hostess who was sadly missed in the Dade City area. William and the other passenger survived to vividly recall the fateful accident that changed their lives. Some say that the tracks are haunted by a number of victims, and the energy of the trains and the heavy steel holds onto the energy.

Silvery Hair Spiraling in the Autumn Breeze in Lacoochee

An accomplished researcher on Native American lore, Robert Shane Forrester painstakingly collected artifacts for many years. His array of tools and utensils from several generations of indigenous people is breathtaking and well-chronicled. Axes, arrowheads and utensils hint at the innovative repurposing from the tribes dating to 10,000 BCE to accommodate warriors involved in the Seminole Wars. (Shane allowed the author to display pieces of his collection at a talk at the Tampa Bay History Center.)

Shane remembered Paul Rogers, in 1987, at a place called Howard's Bar, a remnant of the heyday of Lacoochee, where the likes of Merritt's Grocery, Maples Barbershop and Abe's Drug lined a section of State Road 575 adjacent to rail tracks. Passenger trains that were serviced by two major railroad companies and railcars loaded with cypress logs stood on the rails in the 1950s. There, Shane encountered lively octogenarian Rogers, a clever storyteller, who disclosed an encounter with his great-grandfather James White. White relocated from South Carolina to Pasco County, settling near Lacoochee and assembling a cabin that stood near Cummer Cypress Mill. White's beloved mother later passed away and was laid to rest at the family plot nearby. Weeks after her death, White glimpsed a silver flicker through an opening in the cabin wall and poked a forked oak stick through the crack to capture a glimmering silver hair fluttering in the breeze. White was mesmerized because he recognized it as his deceased mother's hair. The

Some say there is a haunted forest at the Richloam section of the Withlacoochee State Forest near Lacoochee. *Ernest E. Wise.*

The misty fog and the heavily wooded area of Withlacoochee State Forest look enticing. *Ernest E. Wise.*

silvery hair twisted in the gentle breeze in a rhythmic spiral, and he felt the urgency of a forewarning, as hair represented the earth and its protective grasses in Indian culture—a physical extension of thoughts and armor to defeat evil. Rogers paused and then related that his great-grandfather was summoned soon thereafter to war as an infantry sergeant against the Seminoles in 1841.

Hauntings in Withlacoochee Forest and Green Swamp

Twenty-seven-year-old Lacoochee native Evan Green said that all of Lacoochee was at one time occupied by Native Americans who left behind a residual energy that is poignantly felt when roaming the deep woods.

"Those woods are not a safe place to be at night," explained Green as he described a 2010 ghostly encounter at the Richloam Tract of the southeast corner of the Withlacoochee State Forest that is seared in his memory. The only way into the tract was via a winding dirt road that originated a few miles north of Lacoochee.

A Haunted History of Pasco County

Green and six of his buddies came upon a deserted set of buildings deep in the forest. This was a facility opened with funding from a federal grant in November 1978. It was known as a STOP camp for juvenile offenders. Based on an age-old concept that came from the Civilian Conservation Corps of the 1930s, the philosophy was to join troubled teens with the great outdoors and foster work ethic. For a group of no more than twenty boys from ages thirteen to nineteen, a short-term program was to employ the teens in projects around the forest. First opened with a few Quonset huts, it grew to include a cafeteria, classroom, administrative office and sleeping quarters that lay abandoned.

Over time, the program went from housing teens with misdemeanors to a majority with felony convictions. Judge L.R. Huffstetler Jr. said, "STOP is getting children they are not capable of controlling" and cited thirteen juveniles who escaped from the facility in 1983 alone. Later, funding dips from the state caused a shutdown in 2002, followed by the services being contracted to a private agency in 2003 to reopen and a conviction of staff abuse in 2005.

Green said Lacoochee was the nearest location to the STOP camp, although there seemed to be a veil of secrecy. The camp has been bulldozed since the discovery and was replaced by a campground. His encounter in 2010 was ghostly in nature. He and his buddies theorized that an apparition that they encountered was of one of the troubled juveniles haunting the facility. While traveling through the area since then, Green encountered a camper at the location of the previous camp who told him that several fellow campers left abruptly in the middle of the night. Green figured it was the unhappy ghost of the young inmate again.

Folks still talk about the myth of the Green Swamp wild man, which was set into motion in 1974 when Hu Tu-Mei left Taiwan for the United States. He became violently seasick and disoriented on the freighter passage, and while waiting to be flown home, he escaped to the Green Swamp, where he lived for many years. Police and hunters reported seeing the wild man for many years. Resilient, he survived by eating armadillos and foraging, even eating the corn that the game department put out for the turkeys, until 1991.

13
Trilby Tales

A pioneer settlement that thrived with the growth of the railroad came to fruition in the 1870s. First known as McLeod, for one of the pioneer families, the village adopted the name Macon as new settlers from Macon Station, Alabama, favored the new moniker. By 1895, Henry Plant acquired the Orange Belt Railway, which passed through Macon, and converted the narrow-gauge rails to standard rail, and soon, several rails passed through thriving Macon. The name was changed to Trilby in the midst of the release of George DeMaurier's mysterious novel *Trilby*, a story of Bohemian life and hypnotism. Legend has it that Henry Plant's wife convinced him to change the name of the town. In the novel, Svengali is the evil man who exploits Trilby, a young Irish girl, and launches her career as a famous singer. The romantic name of Trilby lingers, and little wonder—there are ghostly stories here.

"Souls in Danger at Trilby"

By Scott Black

The late Earl DeWitt Tyer told an amusing story about a Sunday morning experience at the old Trilby Baptist Church. The Trilby Baptist Church indeed felt like an old building, not as much in actual years but due to its prolonged construction. The cornerstone was laid for the structure in early 1914, under the leadership of Reverend J.M. Lewis. By the end of the year, the congregation moved from the adjoining rude wooden church into the unfinished structure, but full completion came to a standstill.

Unlike other buildings in the community, it was to be a stone block edifice, complete with a belfry, surely intended to make a statement about the status of the Baptists in Trilby. As work slowly moved along, however, the project began to resemble the Lord's parable of the tower builder who didn't count the cost.

Much of the construction was completed by church volunteers. Through the next several years, the church would attract and then lose a string of preachers. Trilby news items in the *Dade City Banner* and the *Florida Baptist Witness* mentioned bursts of new energy that would bring about interior plastering and painting, wiring the building for electricity and even the decision to add two classrooms to the uncompleted building.

Finally, in March 1923, Reverend G.A. Martin and the congregation were able to invite former pastor Reverend J.M. Lewis to come back from Tampa to help dedicate the completed building.

As Earl related his story, it was just before the minister ascended into the pulpit that fateful Sunday that the Baptist members felt the security of the divine hand come down upon them. They had just finished singing the old

The 1914 Trilby Baptist Church. *Scott Black.*

favorite hymn "Love Lifted Me" when a section of the precariously mounted heavy modern lights suddenly snapped from the old ceiling beams and fell down onto the pews below.

Amazingly, none of the assembled church members were injured, and after a few moments of dusting-off and giving thanks for their safety, someone in the group remembered, with a chuckle, a prominent line from the song they had all just been singing: "Souls in danger, look above!"

As the Baptists in Trilby wiped their brows and went home to their Sunday dinners of fried chicken and green beans, they surely uttered more words of appreciation. Yes, in keeping with lyrics from the treasured hymn, "by His love," they had all been saved that day, not "out of the angry waves" but rather by the more appropriate warning to "look above" for the danger of falling objects!

Haunted House of Trilby

Martha Black Sutherland wrote a column for the *Pasco News* for many years that was titled Between Fact & Fancy. To peruse her columns is a real treat. It is reminiscent of the homespun wisdom of Will Rogers. For the April 6, 1978 column, she penned a delightful story about her family's very own haunted home. Dewey and Evy Greene had previously lived in the home, which was known locally as the Dewey Greene place. Martha substituted the aliases of Willie and Myrtle, unaware that the Greene family, who had moved to northern Florida, possessed a newspaper subscription and would spy the article and sound off a bit.

> *Considered the haunted house of Trilby I am sure the collection of ghosts that has stalked the rooms of this house would make an interesting group. We understand the house served as the town tavern for a while. During one period, the post office was the front room, and the postmaster lived upstairs. In the process of doing yard work, we have found a brick foundation on the side of the house. This hints of a fireplace from earlier times. It may have been used by a visiting witch as she stirred her cauldron and sang a song about her double toil and trouble. Also, there is a wide brick foundation about two feet deep in the front yard. Oldtimers around here say there was a line of homes here many years ago.*

Our family has never seen a ghoul sitting around the place, but I have wondered about a couple of books that have completely disappeared. There are strange noises occasionally, but we always attribute these to the settling of the poor old house. It must be rough accommodating our young family. However, there was an incident several years ago. It happened to some earlier residents. I dare say that for a moment serious belief in household ghosts was entertained....

Myrtle [actually Evy] *likes suspense programs on the radio and Willie* [Dewey] *likes practical jokes. It seems the radio was offering a scary story this particular day, and Myrtle was sitting on the edge of her chair right next to the radio so as not to miss a word. Willie was upstairs, but he could hear the radio and knew Myrtle was being held spellbound to the story which was working toward a frightening climax. Willie decided to have some fun. He pulled a sheet over his head and quietly made his way down the stairs toward the completely unsuspecting, shuddering Myrtle. Now as the custom with Myrtle she was in full dress including high spike heel shoes, but Willie had no reason to be concerned with this detail. As he cleared the stairway and approached Myrtle, the perfect time to make a ghostly moan presented itself. Myrtle's blood pressure had probably never been higher as she jerked around and caught sight of the horrifying visitor. With that sight, she jumped up from her chair, collided with Willie who had become entangled in his sheet and had fallen to the floor. Recovering from the encounter, Myrtle, still anxious to get out of the house, took one giant step towards the door and stepped right in the middle of poor Willie's stomach with one of those spike heels.*

Unfortunately, I never heard the end of that story...such as how long did Myrtle stay away from the haunted house, and did Willie suffer from a tummy puncture. But Willie, who asked for his troubles, probably began a pre-joke inspection of Myrtle's feet after that.

Still owned by Martha, the Dewey Greene place has a long history and was occupied by many. It was moved to Trilby from Lenard on the Orange Belt Railway in 1904 by William S. Kuster, the postmaster.

14
Moon Lake

The Dude Ranch

Moon Lake's Transformations

Bejeweled with magnificent splendor and lavish resources, Moon Lake was also a favored area in antiquity but was rediscovered by pioneers as a rendezvous for sportsmen. Newspaper social columns boasted abundant bass fishing excursions, hunting and camping in the opulent 1920s. The *Times* recounted that Tampa mayor Horace C. Gordon, while at Moon Lake, cooked cornbread and fried fish and then acted as caller for several dances as campers brought along a Victrola. It stated, "Besides being a good mayor, he is an excellent cook."

The *Tarpon Springs Leader* announced that the Moon Lake Lodge debuted in 1933 as a twelve-thousand-acre project, an enterprise of Clearwater's Ed Haley, who poured out $600,000.

Haley created a rustic paradise/dude ranch with thirty-five thousand rose bushes, azaleas, red magnolias, japonicas and palms. In the game preserve, Haley put one thousand Virginia and English fallow deer enclosed by a seventeen-mile, eight-foot-high fence. African partridges, wild turkeys, quail, ducks and Indian and Java peafowl roamed the preserve, and a stable of horses with miles of horse trails meandered the grounds. At night, the two-hundred-acre lake was circled with yellow, red and blue lights.

A sixty-foot-long bar adorned the casino—even during Prohibition—and all guests were cleared upon entry. Baseball great Babe Ruth and elites like

Entering Moon Lake Lodge during Prohibition meant getting clearance at the gate. *State Archives of Florida.*

Joseph Kennedy and Cornelius Vanderbilt, as well as Hollywood actresses Gloria Swanson, Lana Turner and Lillian Gish, were guests at Moon Lake Lodge. With gambling and bootleg liquor, the festive park was said to be a favorite haunt of Chicago mafia, including Al Capone, although the assertion of Capone's visit has been discredited by several historians.

"It's not inconceivable that after Capone got out of prison in 1939, he was at Moon Lake," said historian Dayton. "West Pasco certainly would have fit the bill in those days." Weighing in, Midge London-Prace said the West Pasco Historical Society found no proof of his visit. Still, she said, "People love this juicy piece of folklore."

Moon Lake declined in the Great Depression and World War II, and attempts to reinvent it included a Baptist church camp. Unfortunately, in September 1996, the deteriorating lodge was the victim of arson by a sixteen-year-old girl, who pleaded no contest to the charge.

As for the Capone theory, two other notorious gangsters, Alva Hunt and Hugo Grant, who came out of Sumter County during the Roaring Twenties, had ties to Pasco and visited the dude ranch.

The gangsters first honed their talents in fencing cars and were apprehended in Pasco in 1927 but turned to the more lucrative bank robberies, train hold-ups and the like. The significant difference between the duo and other gangsters like Capone was their use of minor violence that resulted in no deaths.

In January 1938, they were brought to trial and represented by seasoned Dade City defense attorney George Dayton and his father, O.L. Dayton, along with Clark Gourley. The attorney George Hoffman called twenty-five witnesses for the government, but the defense called none. After the first day of the trial, an apparent agreement was made between Dayton and his team from Dade City for the defendants to defend themselves. It remains a mystery as to why the defense team was dismissed by the gangsters.

15

SAN ANTONIO

RATTLESNAKES AND NUNS

Founded as a Catholic colony by Edmund Francis Dunne, San Antonio was incorporated in 1891. Dunne, a former chief justice of the Arizona Supreme Court, claimed to have experienced an epiphany while lost and received an intercession from Saint Anthony that empowered him to originate a Catholic colony in the name of the saint. The opportunity came when Hamilton Disston, Philadelphia saw-maker, procured from a broker faltering land in Florida. The deal netted Dunne 100,000 acres to realize his dream.

The identity of the area was intertwined with Lake Jovita and St. Leo University, which was dedicated in 1890.

RATTLESNAKE FESTIVAL

Who would have a festival to celebrate a killer?

The mention of a rattlesnake festival creates a chill up your spine. The star of this festival, which debuted in San Antonio, Florida, in 1967 and lasted for fifty-one years, was the eastern diamondback rattlesnake (*Crotalus adamanteus*), a carnivorous reptile that lives from ten to twenty years. It is one of the heaviest venomous snakes in the American continents and is the largest rattlesnake.

Dennie Seebolt gave demonstrations at Rattlesnake Festival. He ran a Snake-A-Torium in Panama City from 1946 until the 1990s and passed away in 2017. *State Archives of Florida.*

Will Post suggested an innovative idea to the local San Antonio Jaycees for a festival to rival Plant City's strawberry festival. A month-long rattlesnake collection took place, and prizes were given for the winning entries—largest snake and most snakes apprehended. Some sixteen years later, co-founder Eddie Herrmann said the festival was well known, if not a bit curious: "We just couldn't get it in the newspaper in 1967; everybody laughed at us." It has now graced the pages of the *London Times*, the *New York Times* and *Southern Living* and has been reported on by the *Tonight Show*.

Records in the snake contest were held by Leo and Lucille Barthle of Darby, who captured over one hundred rattlesnakes through the years. The heaviest was a six-footer, weighing twelve pounds. Hourly snake shows were presented in the early days by Art Bass and later by Dennie Sebolt of the Snake-A-Torium in Panama City Beach.

By 1977, philosophy was changing, and the *Fort Lauderdale News* reported that organizers paid two dollars a foot for every rattlesnake but encouraged locals to not capture the poisonous rattlers. With animal rights issues coming to light, the focus of the festival shifted from the animals to arts and wildlife awareness, and it was relocated to Dade City and repackaged by a nonprofit.

Needless to say, there were more than a few scares as visitors and even residents viewed the phenomenal and haunting eastern diamondback rattlesnakes for which the festival was originated in San Antonio.

The Nun's Murder Tale Took on a Life of Its Own

"I was at the Osceola Bar a few years ago and overheard some St. Leo students talking about the brutal murder of the phantom nun in St. Edwards Hall and shook my head, thinking 'Is that story still alive?'" said Dayton, explaining that when they were students in the class of 1962 at the St. Leo College Preparatory School, he and John Hofstee concocted the tale as a Halloween prank. A complete fantasy, it involved a young nun being abducted and brutally murdered with vivid detail of events and place. "We even put red ink on some stair railing and around campus," he said.

As he was sitting at the Osceola and listening to the recounting of their whopper, he realized the yarn had taken on a life of its own for a few generations. Historian Brian Swann recalled hearing the story of the murdered nun when he was a student at St. Leo University in 1989, recounted to him in graphic detail by female students who, at that time, were housed on the fourth floor of his dormitory.

The same two bartenders at the Osceola Bar also told Dayton that on several occasions, at closing time, each glimpsed the shadowy image of an old man standing at the bar, and as they threw up their arms and gasped, the man vanished.

16
ELLERSLIE AND ENTERPRISE

Ellerslie was first settled in 1883, according to the *Florida State Gazetteer*, and was situated on the line of the South Florida Railroad. A Confederate surgeon with the Tenth South Carolina Regiment, James Goodwin Wallace, founded the town in 1881.

SOUNDS FROM THE SANCTUARY OF ENTERPRISE CHURCH

Settlers built the Enterprise Methodist Church in the community of Ellerslie/Enterprise in 1878. Served by a circuit-riding preacher, "fifth-Sunday sings and dinner on the grounds" were commonplace. The building was replaced in 1905 for the cost of $500 and was deeded to the Pioneer Florida Museum and Village in Dade City in 1976 for preservation.

Hedman reported in the *Tribune* on October 26, 2003, in a section titled "Sounds from Sanctuary," that Donna Swart, curator at the museum, and charter member/trustee Lela Futch reported hearing strange sounds coming from the Enterprise Church. After investigation, it was determined that there were no radios playing and nothing to explain what they heard. Swart, who was a mayor of San Antonio, was museum curator at a time of tremendous growth from 1990 to 2005, and Futch was active in numerous civic organizations.

The pioneer Enterprise Church has been a hands-on exhibit at the Pioneer Florida Museum & Village since 1977. *Ernest E. Wise.*

Mary Lee Madill Parsons shared tales of Ellerslie with Stephanie Black, director of the Pioneer Florida Museum & Village. *Author's collection.*

Yellow Lining from Yellow Jackets

Mary Lee Madill Parsons lived by the adage "enjoy every day as a blessing." She said her philosophy of life originated from her early days. Her family migrated to Ellerslie in 1918. The family rented a small boxcar and arrived at a tiny depot in 1918, and Mary was born in Ellerslie in 1922.

For the 140th anniversary of the Enterprise Church, which stood in Ellerslie and is now an exhibit at the Pioneer Florida Museum & Village, director Stephanie Black collected stories about the pioneer church and interviewed Mary Lee. Mary Lee had attended school in the church. "Enterprise church was always packed on Sundays and busy with horse and buggies all about," she shared. The community was close-knit, and everyone looked out for one another. Even the train conductor would sound a particular whistle pattern to her father if a cow or hog had been hit on the track so that he would know to go and retrieve the meat for a family, explained Mary Lee.

The church was surrounded by the cemetery, where the practice was for the entire grave to be covered by concrete. With the school so close to the cemetery, students ate lunch outside and would sit on top of a tombstone. Mary Lee shared:

> *I remember the time that a baby passed away, and my parents came to the rescue. My father constructed a little coffin from wood, and my mother lined the coffin with delicate material from a yellow jacket for the burial. Sometime later, I remember playing in the cemetery and encountering a wicked swarm of yellow jackets—of fourteen or fifteen stings—and as I was coming out of the daze, there was a gentleman, perhaps the doctor, dotting me with tobacco juice, which was the custom for treating stings. He was literally spitting tobacco on the bites to soothe the effect of the razor blade–like stings. Sure is strange what comes to mind….the yellow lining of the coffin and the yellow jackets—makes you wonder.*

Mary Lee and her husband went on to work for Pan American Airlines during the days when Eddie Rickenbacker was at the helm of Eastern Airlines, and they traveled extensively throughout the world with their travel vouchers but always thought longingly of Ellerslie as their home.

BIBLIOGRAPHY

Abrams, Rick. "Lewis Van Dercar May Change His Style of Living—in 100 Years." *Tampa Bay Times*, May 16, 1978.

Allman, John M. "Hunting for the Real Ghosts of 'Scream-A-Geddon' in Dade City." *Creative Loafing: Tampa Bay*, October 10, 2019.

Arellano, Chris. "Aging Cinema Comes Alive with Plays, Musicals." *Tampa Tribune*, July 15, 1991.

Austin, Robert J. Assessment Report of Pasadena Hills, Tampa. Southeastern Archaeological Research, Inc, Search Project No. 2427-09031, August 2009.

Barnesville News-Gazette. "Tribute to Mr. Overstreet." August 24, 1922.

Bentley, Cheryl. "New Port Richey Book Is Surprise Best Seller." *Tampa Bay Tribune*, April 28, 2005.

Beyer, Mark. "Ghosts Enliven History Tour." *Tampa Tribune*, May 27, 2005.

———. "Theater Produces Stories of Spirit." *Tampa Tribune*, May 23, 2005.

Black, Martha. Between Fact & Fancy. *Pasco News*, April 6, 1978.

Black, Scott internet interview with author. Pasco County, FL. July 16, 2020.

Blalock, Bill. "Pasco Lived with 'Road to Nowhere' for Decade." *Tampa Tribune*, January 1, 1961.

Bostick, Susanne. "Chasco Fiesta Benefits Entire County." *Tampa Tribune*, February 27, 1975.

Bowen, Charles T. "Ghost Tales Never Hurt Bottom Line." *Tampa Tribune*, October 31, 1995.

Bradford Telegraph. "At Random—News from All Parts of the State Summarized." May 17, 1895.

Bibliography

Brainard, Jeffrey. "Aging Landmark Is at Home Again." *Tampa Bay Times*, June 17, 1996.
Brown, Rosemary. "Archaeologist Finds Culture of Indians in Grassy Knolls." *Tampa Tribune*, January 26, 1983.
———. "Spooky Tales." *Tampa Tribune*, October 21, 1984.
Bullen, Ripley P. "S.T. Walker, an Early Florida Archaeologist." *Florida Anthropologist* 4, no. 3–4 (November 1951): 46–49.
Cannon, Jeff. "Temple Mound a Monument to Pasco's Native History." Patch Media. September 1, 2011. patch.com.
Capuzzo, Mike. "Grave Affair." *Miami Herald*, October 25, 1981.
Carley, Ruby. "Sun God Memorial in Safe Hands." *Tampa Bay Times*, March 17, 1970.
Carozza, Adam J. "New Port Richey: Myth and History of a City Built on Enchantment." University of South Florida, 2009.
Chastain, Shirley. "Fort Dades Remembered." *Tampa Bay Times*, April 2, 1967.
Chattanooga Daily Times. "Five Murderers Will Hang." October 7, 1894.
Collins, Ronald phone interview with author. Pasco County, FL. January 29, 2020.
Dade City Banner. "Dade City History Is Reviewed." August 17, 1928.
———. "Deputy Finds Recluse Dead in Zephyrhills." August 15, 1952.
———. "Ivey Overstreet Proves Alibi." August 20, 1915.
———. "John O'Berry Is Foully Murdered." November 12, 1915.
———. "Mrs. Winifred B. Latham Obituary." April 18, 1963.
———. "Negro Brute Foully Assaulted Woman and Made Escape." June 30, 1916.
———. "Negro Pays Penalty with Life When Trilby Mob Breaks in Jail." August 6, 1915.
———. "Portia I. Fordyce Obituary." December 5, 1957.
———. "Sheriff Kills Will Hyatt in Self-Defense." July 9, 1915.
———. "Three War Heroes Die Within Day." May 12, 1922.
———. "Tom Scott and Elmore Tucker, of Richland, Shot from Ambush." August 6, 1915.
———. "250 German Prisoners Arrived Here Tuesday." April 14, 1944.
———. "Where Is This Haunted House?" July 13, 1926.
Day, Phyllis. "Haunted Trails and Other Scares Kick Off Halloween." *Tampa Bay Times*, October 18, 2019.
Dayton, William, Esq., interview with author. Zephyrhills, Pasco County, FL. February 4 and 27, 2020.

Bibliography

De Vaugondy, Gilles Robert. *La Floride, Divisée en Floride et Caroline*. Paris: G. Robert de Vaugondy, 1749.

Florida Peninsular. "Army News—R.D. Bradley." August 29, 1857.

Fort Myers Press. "Dade City Proves Princely Host to Press Association." October 6, 1924.

Fox, Geoff. "Moon Lake Paradise Lost." *Tampa Tribune*, May 16, 2010.

Frank, Joe. "Lights! Camera! Action! Big Bucks!" *Tampa Bay Times*, April 15, 1990.

Fredricksen, Barbara. "Attention Ghost: Exit Stage Left, through Wall." *Tampa Bay Times*, October 31, 2006.

———. "The Theater to Be." *Tampa Bay Times*, August 12, 1994.

Freeman, Erica internet interview/consultation with author. Zephyrhills, FL. February 12 and 20, 2020.

Furman, Simon. "Very Latest—Two of Captain Bradley's Children Killed." *Peninsular*, May 17, 1856.

Glamsch, Panky. "Crystal Springs—A Mid Florida Shangri-la." *Tampa Tribune*, February 12, 1976.

———. "Hudson Cemetery Houses Burial Site of Early Indians." *Tampa Tribune*, October 2, 1975.

Glidewell, Jan. "The Elegance of Yesterday Reborn." *Tampa Bay Times*, June 28, 1976.

———. "Ghostbusting Isn't So Tough." *Tampa Bay Times*, July 6, 1986.

———. "Larger Than Life." *Tampa Bay Times*, December 26, 1988.

———. "A Look Back at When Bodies Were Dumped in Pasco." *Tampa Bay Times*, October 5, 1982.

Grumet, Bridget Hall. "Legend of Al Capone's Hideaway Won't Go Away." *Tampa Bay Times*, April 24, 2005.

Gude, Joe phone interview with author. Pasco County, FL. March 12, 2020.

Hall, Alice. "Cemetery Said Oldest in Pasco—Family Burying Ground Scene of Annual Reunion." *Tampa Tribune*, June 15, 1963.

Hall, Kenneth. "Pasco Region Entertainer Has Flavor for Florida Taste." *Tampa Tribune*, November 9, 2006.

Heagney, John. "Theater Is Testament of Hope for Regional Arts." *Tampa Times*, August 10, 1980.

Heagney, John, and Willard Clark. "Major Force in Local Theater, Dies at 74." *Tampa Bay Times*, June 5, 1981.

———. "Richey Suncoast Theatre President Dies." *Tampa Bay Times*, June 25, 1981.

Bibliography

Hedman, Carol Jeffares. "An Abused Woman Fought Back." *Tampa Tribune*, November 6, 2005.

———. "Crystal Springs Has Murky Past." *Tampa Tribune*, May 21, 2002.

———. "Darby Is the Site of Last Settler-Indian Conflict." *Tampa Tribune*, October 15, 1983.

———. "Diverse Groups Called Lake Pasadena Home." *Tampa Tribune*, May 4, 2003.

———. "Faded Cemetery Speaks to History." *Tampa Tribune*, September 17, 2004.

———. "Fire Destroys House with Haunted Past." *Tampa Tribune*, December 10, 1989.

———. "Former Timber Town of Odessa Keeps an Eye on Past." *Tampa Tribune*, December 14, 2003.

———. "A Fortune in Gossip Was Found." *Tampa Tribune*, July 29, 1989.

———. "Freezes Finished Lakefront Community." *Tampa Tribune*, January 9, 2000.

———. "Historical Structures Cast a Broad Shadow in City." *Tampa Tribune*, October 17, 2003.

———. "Home Haunted for Spook & Lawyer." *Tampa Tribune*, October 26, 2002.

———. "Hotels Have Storied Tradition in West Pasco." *Tampa Tribune*, December 21, 1985.

———. "If the Walls Could Speak, the Stories." *Tampa Tribune*, May 25, 1989.

———. "Lawyer Has a Ghost Story to Tell." *Tampa Tribune*, October 26, 2003.

———. "Man Recounts Different Kind of Dade History." *Tampa Tribune*, May 30, 1987.

———. "New Port Richey Miscast in Role as Hollywood East." *Tampa Tribune*, January 2, 2004.

———. "Pasco Once Known as Pleasant Plains." *Tampa Tribune*, September 19, 2002.

———. "Sawmills Helped." *Tampa Tribune*, January 1, 2002.

———. "There Are Many Haunting Tales of This Old House in Zephyrhills." *Tampa Tribune*, May 7, 1997.

———. "Trailblazing Hotels Lured Early Tourists." *Tampa Tribune*, November 7, 2003.

———. "Winnie Was Destined to Be Lonely." *Tampa Tribune*, March 30, 1985.

Bibliography

Hernando Sun. "The Bradley Massacre: Last Such Attack East of Mississippi." May 19, 2017.

Herrmann, Edward, Horgan James and Alice Hall. *The Historic Places of Pasco County*. Dade City, FL: Pasco County Historical Press, 1992.

Holland, George. "Thomas Meighan Buys Land & Plans Winter Home in New Port Richey at Once." *Tampa Tribune*, February 25, 1926.

Hopkins, Carolyn. "The Show Goes On." *Tampa Bay Times*, July 29, 1985.

Hutchinson Daily World. "Four to Hang." October 7, 1894.

Jackson, Tom. "There Ought to Be a Law About Making Dumb Laws." *Tampa Tribune*, May 23, 2012.

Jeter, Jeff phone interview with author. Pasco County, FL. March 13, 2020.

Jewell, Lorie. "Couple Brings New Life to Old House." *Tampa Tribune*, July 19, 1992.

———. "Ghost Has Theater Seat." *Tampa Tribune*, October 31, 2006.

Johnson, Ted interview with author at Hugh Embry Library. Dade City, FL. January 28, 2020.

Kalfas, Marilyn. "Mr. Theater Gets Results." *Tampa Tribune*, May 27, 1980.

Key West Citizen. "Florinda Medina Dies; Demise Recalls Tale of Weird Love Affair." July 12, 1946.

———. "He's Sane, Declares Board after Hearing." October 10, 1940.

———. "Hold Van Cosel on Malicious and Wanton Charges." October 7, 1940.

———. "Van Cosel Case Was Dismissed." November 11, 1940.

Kladko, Brian. "Dade City Has Had Its Share of Dark Days." *Tampa Bay Times*, June 2, 1989.

Kleinberg, Eliot. "Undying Love." *Palm Beach Post*, October 29, 1995.

Knight, Dick. "Polter—A Spooky Mrs. Fix It—For Sale." *Miami Herald*, July 3, 1961.

Knoxville Tribune. "Brutal Florida Murder." September 19, 1894.

Kornacki, Steve. "Oasis of Creativity." *Tampa Tribune*, August 1, 2005.

Kovel, Terry. "Beware of Spirits Affixed to Antiques." *Tampa Tribune*, October 28, 2011.

Krug, Karl. "Frances Ring's Death Writes an Ending to Meighan Love Story." *Pittsburgh Sun Telegraph*, January 18, 1951.

Lagosky, Leslie Gilmore interview with author. Zephyrhills, Pasco County, FL. February 4 and 7, 2020, and March 6, 2020.

Lipper, Hal. "Sharp View of Suburbia." *Tampa Bay Times*, December 14, 1990.

Los Angeles Times. "Mrs. Meighan, Silent Star's Widow Dies." January 16, 1951.

Bibliography

Mach, William. "Eccentric Left Behind a Trail of Controversy." *Tampa Tribune*, June 1, 1986.

MacManus, Elizabeth. "Stagecoach." *Tampa Bay Times*, September 10, 1995.

Martinez, Christopher. "Museum Curator Finds Cigar Smoke Smell Haunting." *Tampa Tribune*, September 6, 2002.

Mase, Same. "Cotee Adds Charm to New Port Richey." *Tampa Daily Times*, July 25, 1946.

McMillian, Susan interview with author. Dade City, Pasco County, FL. March 1 and 15, 2020.

McGavern, Edith phone interview with author. Zephyrhills, Pasco County, FL. January 29, 2020.

McQuikin, Steve. "Pasco Residents Get a Silver Screen Thrill." *Tampa Tribune*, December 14, 1990.

Miami Daily News. "Death Ends Case of Dr. von Cosel." August 14, 1952.

Miami News. "Oil Paintings by Van Dercar to Be Shown." April 9, 1950.

Miller, Michele. "Entrepreneurial Spirits: Could Paranormal Tourism Be the Next Big Attraction in New Port Richey?" *Tampa Bay Times*, July 19, 2019.

———. "Returning to Glory." *Tampa Bay Times*, September 27, 2019.

Neil, Wilfred T. "Crystal Springs Once Was Hold for Ice Age Beast." *Tampa Bay Times*, November 11, 1979.

Ocala Evening Star. "Capture Suspects in Pasco County." October 7, 1922.

Orth, Carl. "Lakeside Inn Owner Expressed Interest in Hacienda." *Suncoast News*, March 14, 2018.

———. "Landmark Hacienda Takes Center Stage." *Tampa Tribune*, October 30, 2015.

Osborne, Tish. "Civil War Letter Found in Desk at Historical Museum." *Tampa Tribune*, August 2, 2002.

Palm Beach Post. "Magic City Loses Roc Egg Maker, Lewis Van Dercar." September 26, 1973.

———. "So This Is Florida? The New Klondike with Thomas Meighan." March 14, 1926.

Panama City News-Herald. "Kept Woman's Body Seven Years." October 9, 1940.

———. "Man Who Kept Body of Woman He Loved Eight Years Is Dead." August 14, 1952.

Pensacola News. "Slew His Unfaithful Wife." August 22, 1894.

Post-Standard. "Chiefs to Train at Dade City, Florida." December 17, 1961.

Pounds, Geoffrey. "Winifred Bridge Knew of Beauty, Life, Tragedy." *Tampa Tribune*, July 28, 1980.

Bibliography

———. "Years After Seminole Wars Ended, Indians Still Sought Retribution." *Tampa Tribune*, December 15, 1980.
Rabiroff, Jon. "Going Hollywood." *Tampa Tribune*, April 28, 1990.
Ross, Bob. "Cutting Edge Fairy Tale." *Tampa Tribune*, December 14, 1990.
Shopenhauer, Arthur. *The Wisdom of Life*. London: Swan Sonnenshein & Company, 1890.
Smith, Anne. "Grave Robbery a Halloween Tale of Horrors." *Miami Tribune*, November 2, 1971.
Smith, Katherine Snow. "New Luster Planned for an Old Landmark." *Tampa Bay Times*, June 23, 1996.
Spencer, Camille C. "Developer Plans to Preserve Cemetery." *Tampa Bay Times*, June 22, 2007.
———. "A Ghostly Town? Is It Truly a Ghostly Town?" *Tampa Bay Times*, October 31, 2009.
Stiles, Sandy. "Dade Massacre—Bloodiest Page." *Tampa Bay Times*, October 19, 1952.
Stoddard, Missy. "Doorway to Historic Restoration." *Tampa Tribune*, August 5, 2003.
Sullivan, Erin. "A Ghost or Hoax? Group Says Voice on Tape Is of Civil War Man." *Tampa Bay Times*, July 9, 2009.
———. "A Ghost—Or Hoax?" *Tampa Bay Times*, July 16, 2009.
Tampa Bay Times. "Builders Are Landmarks to Colorful Past." April 12, 1987.
———. "City's Jailhouse Walls Have Tales to Tell." July 12, 1999.
———. "Gildard Seeks Clemency for 120." November 21, 1937.
———. "A New Shrine for a Vulnerable Home." October 9, 1995.
———. "Pasco County Sales Booming." March 22, 1925.
———. "Plaque Honors Willard Clark." November 21, 1981.
———. "Shell Mound Property Sold & Improved." March 27, 1925.
———. "St. Pete Crowd Returns from 4 Day Fishing Trip to Moon Lake." August 8, 1920.
———. "Theatre Built of Dense Pine—Thomas Meighan Showhouse Boosts New Port Richey." July 10, 1926.
———. "Work Planned on Road to Nowhere." March 10, 1966.
Tampa Daily News. "State Social News—Zephyrhills Has Real Museum." February 21, 1914.
Tampa Daily Times. "Will Discuss Market Plans." August 10, 1917.
Tampa Morning Tribune. "B.D. Sturkie, Pioneer in Pasco County, Dies." November 7, 1928.
———. "Crystal Springs." April 19, 1919.

Bibliography

———. "Dade City Posses After Young Negro-Brutal Attack on Mrs. Braswell." July 28, 1916.
———. "Old Ghosts Home Burns to Ground." December 16, 1937.
———. "Professor Morris—South Florida Social Notes." July 26, 1914.
———. "Rockefeller Adds 17,000 Acres to Florida Holdings." October 26, 1926.
———. "Speeder's Paradise." August 9, 1926.
———. "Try to Scare Blacks Away from Dade City." July 28, 1916.
———. "Widow of Eccentric Zephyrhills Man to Settle Estate." October 31, 1952.
Tampa Sunday Tribune. A.B. Morris Obituary. July 25, 1915.
———. "Coleman's Statement of Dade City Affair." July 9, 1916.
———. "German War Prisoners Get Fat in Florida." May 14, 1944.
———. "Little Theatre Player—Willard Clark." May 16, 1954.
Tampa Tribune. "Able Lawyer Life Is Over—Judge Barron Phillips." May 3, 1904.
———. "ACL Train Is Derailed Near Odessa." January 21, 1937.
———. "Bloodhounds and Posse Seeking Negro." July 2, 1916.
———. "Complicity in Three Murders Charged Against Ellis." June 29, 1907.
———. "Dade City Woman Held in Jail for Murder of Two Men." May 26, 1935.
———. "The Day the Elevator Stuck." September 4, 1979.
———. "Diseased Prisoner Saws Way from Jail." December 22, 1923.
———. "Efforts of Florida Man Led to Famous Song." January 30, 1917.
———. "Famous Millionaires of Broadway Buy in New Port Richey." January 3, 1926.
———. "First Photos of German War Prisoners in Florida Canneries." May 14, 1944.
———. "Funeral Notice for Mrs. Doris A. Tanzler." May 11, 1977.
———. "Gerkin Held for Robbery in Lacoochee." July 14, 1923.
———. "Hudson Physician Sought in New Orleans." February 17, 1909.
———. "Lake View Hotel Burned to Ground." January 1, 1902.
———. "Land O'Lakes: Drexel, Denham United Under New Name." June 17, 1949.
———. "Many Communities Dot Lake Region of Pasco." November 30, 1941.
———. "New Hotel Opens in Tourist Town: Hacienda." February 6, 1927.
———. "Odessa Is Town of Fairy Tale Big Movie Studio to Be Built." December 3, 1925.

Bibliography

———. "Rebirth of a Theater." May 12, 1972.
———. "Sculptor Lewis Van Der Car—Man Creates Live-In Enchanted Forest." February 15, 1974.
———. "Sheriff Here Today." August 6, 1914.
———. "Sheriff Kills Hite." July 6, 1915.
———. "Structure to Be Beautified." July 12, 1925.
———. "Woman Tells Why She Killed Two Pasco Men." May 19, 1935.
———. "Zukor, Ed Wynn, Gene Buck, Cohan & Others Send Good Wishes." July 2, 1926.
Tampa Weekly Tribune. "Hangman to Reap a Harvest in Pasco County—Judge Phillips Sentences Five Murderers to Swing." October 12, 1894.
———. "Odessa Center of a Smiling Region." August 24, 1911.
———. "Report of Murder at Ehren Reaches City." July 7, 1909.
Tanno, Jessica. "Story of Area Indians Come Alive." *Tampa Bay Times*, March 11, 1998.
Taylor, Carl B. "Bradley Massacre at Darby in 1856." *Dade City Banner*, August 4, 1922.
———. "High Hill in Pasco County Got Name from Tragedy in Bygone Day of Mail Coach." *Tampa Tribune*, January 16, 1927.
Temple, John. "Rezoning Near Dade City Gets Go-Ahead from County." *Tampa Tribune*, April 21, 1999.
Thompson, Bill. "Back in Time." *Tampa Tribune*, April 19, 1998.
Thorner, James. "The City's Old Jailhouse Walls Have Tales to Tell." *Tampa Bay Times*, July 12, 1991.
———. "On the Trail of Ancient People." *Tampa Bay Times*, February 24, 2004.
Walker, S.T. "Preliminary Explorations Among the Indian Mounds in South Florida." *Annual Report of Smithsonian Institute for 1879* (1879): 392–412.
Ware, Lucy. "Guests Routed by Hotel Fire." *Tampa Bay Times*, June 7, 1968.
Westermann, Eileen Ann phone interview with author. Dade City, FL. March 13, 2020.
Whitney, Elizabeth. "Moon Lake Metamorphosis—Gambler's Haunt to Church Retreat." *Tampa Bay Times*, July 6, 1963.
Wilson, Chip. "Historical Site Is Missing Its Marker." *Tampa Tribune*, October 12, 1984.
Wilson, Dale. "Something Strange Is Bound to Occur in Every Town." *Tampa Bay Times*, August 26, 1977.
Woodcock, Nell. "Port Richey Opens 50th Anniversary Celebration Today." *Tampa Bay Times*, May 18, 1975.

About the Author

Madonna Jervis Wise delights in writing and riding. She is a lifelong historian and genealogist. She served as a school principal, teacher, counselor and district school administrator in three Florida school districts. With a bachelor of arts in history from Taylor University and a master of science in counselor education and school administration from the University of South Florida, she holds credentials as a licensed mental health counselor and grant institute certification in Florida.

A Haunted History of Pasco County is her first venture into a new genre; however, her previous writing has been diverse, from curriculums and federal grants in academia to published fiction, nonfiction, historical accounts and newspaper journalism. She has previously authored several books, including three local Florida histories for Arcadia Publishing.

Madonna enjoys researching family history with her husband, Ernest, also an educator. She is an accomplished equestrian and can often be found on the trail on her beloved Paint/Pinto, Saltwater Cowboy, and she savors time with her three adult children, J. Jervis Wise, Esq.; Mamie V.J. Wise, Esq.; and Rachel Beth Wise, and her glorious grandchildren.